Magic Moments™
Cooking With Your Kids

Written by Patricia A. Staino
Illustrated by Marilynn G. Barr

The Education Center, Inc.
Greensboro, North Carolina

For Mom & Dad, who always played with me....

©1997 by THE EDUCATION CENTER, INC.
All rights reserved except as here noted.

ISBN# 1-65234-173-1

The Education Center, Inc.
Box 9753
Greensboro, NC 27429-0753

Manufactured in the United States
10 9 8 7 6 5 4 3 2 1

COOKING

WITH YOUR KIDS

Table of Contents

Table of Contents

Dear Kids,

It looks like you're ready to discover the fun and excitement of cooking! That's why Mom and Dad brought home this really cool cookbook for you, right? Sure, sure, they think it's a great way to teach you responsibility and for you to learn to do things around the house for yourself. But the truth is, you'll love to cook because you get to play with doughy, pasty, sticky things. You can get a little dirty, and Mom won't mind. You get to play with all kinds of interesting utensils (like spatulas, whisks, and mixing bowls) that are usually out of your reach. Most of all, you get to make the yummy, delicious snacks and meals that you love the most and share them with your family.

Now that you've grown enough to work in the kitchen with Mom and Dad, though, it's time to remember a few simple rules:

- Cooking is fun, but it's not a game. You will be working with things that are hot, sharp, pointy, and electric. Anytime you have to use a knife, an oven, a blender, or a mixer, make sure Mom or Dad is with you.

- If Mom and Dad are trusting you enough to let you start cooking on your own, show them that you CAN be trusted. Listen to their instructions and follow any rules they set up for you. If they tell you to stay out of the kitchen when they are not home, stay out. If you don't listen, you could hurt yourself or your brother or sister.

- Cleaning up is just as much a part of cooking as the mixing and blending. Once you're finished, wash all the dishes, utensils, and countertops.

It looks like you're ready to get started. So tie on your apron, grab your wire whisk and a grown-up, and let's get cookin'!

Dear Mom & Dad,

Before you and your child begin baking and browning and sautéing, take a few moments to read through the introductory pages of this book. This is a resource book for you as well as a cookbook for kids. We've marked the recipes that kids can do alone and the ones that require your supervision. We've made it easy for you and your child to feel at home in your kitchen.

Take the time to sit down with your child and explain your kitchen rules. Make it very clear when he is allowed to cook, who he is allowed to cook with, and what kinds of kitchen tools he may and may not use.

Cooking doesn't just teach kids how to prepare food. By being in the kitchen, your child will practice his reading skills while browsing through cookbooks. He will practice counting, measurement, number-recognition, and fraction skills when he counts out teaspoons of sugar or doubles a recipe. He will learn how to follow directions, particularly in a sequential order, and will see firsthand that there are direct consequences when things are not done correctly. Finally, he will learn about eating, nutrition, and independence. He learns all this, with no coercion to open a textbook!

Now spend some time browsing through the recipes to find out what interests your child and choose something to make tonight!

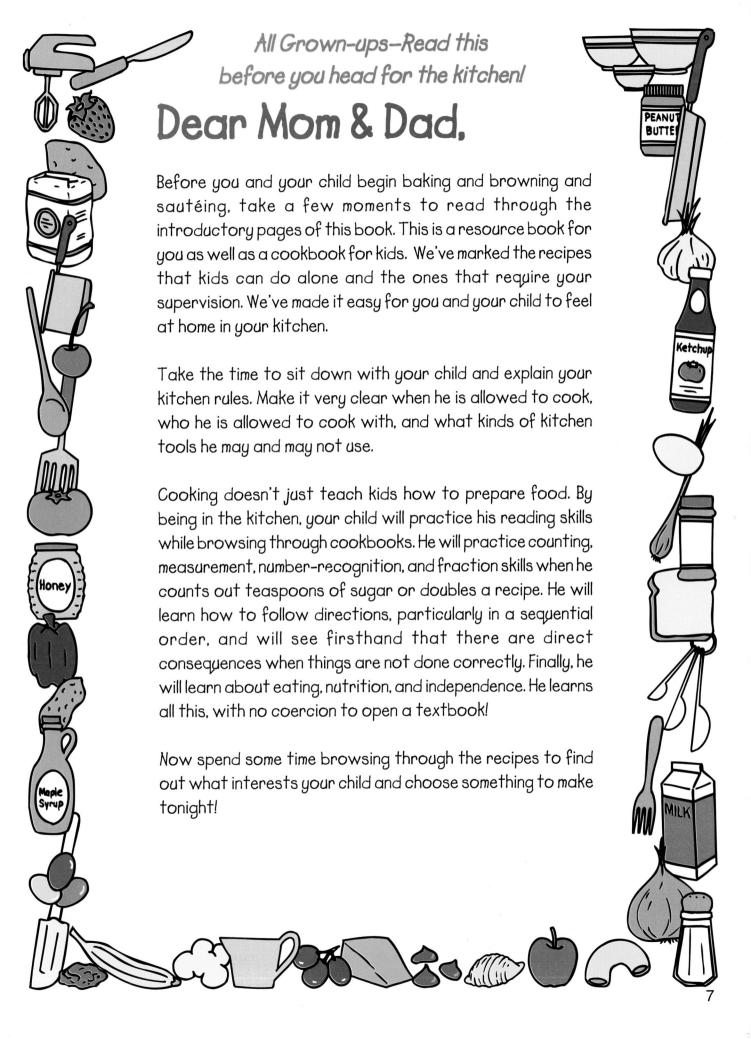

The Cook's Code—How To Use This Book

You will find little pictures next to some steps in the recipes. It's a secret code to make following these recipes a little easier. Before you begin, find out what all these little symbols mean.

 A stop sign means you should be sure there is an adult around to help you. This could mean Mom, Dad, Grandma, the baby-sitter—just about anyone who is allowed to work in the kitchen. Adults are good to have around when you want to use the stovetop or a knife, or when you boil water or drain something into the sink.

Color Words—Sometimes you will find a word that is in color. This word is probably new to you (like *colander* or *spatula*). You can find these words in the glossary at the end of the book. The glossary will explain what the words mean.

 These little chefs' hats rate the recipes. You'll find them on each and every page. They will tell you if the recipe is easy or hard, if you can do it by yourself or if you need an adult. Here's what they mean:

 These are the easiest recipes in the book. You don't need a stove, electric appliances, or a sharp knife. You won't need a lot of ingredients. You can do these all by yourself.

 Something needs to be boiled, baked, microwaved, or drained, so an adult will have to help you for a few minutes. Otherwise, these recipes are pretty simple to make.

 These recipes have only a few ingredients, but you'll need an adult to help. (Mom usually needs to keep an eye on the stove). You may need to use a mixer, a knife, or the oven. Make sure someone who is allowed to use those things is around.

 These are the hardest recipes in the book. They have a lot of ingredients and a lot of steps. These recipes should be saved until you've had some practice in the kitchen. You should wait until Mom or Dad has the time to spend with you while you make the whole recipe.

Munchies & Dips

Munchies and dips are really fun foods. Think about it—when does Mom bring out the dip bowl? On holidays? When company comes? At parties? When you and Dad are watching the Super Bowl?

Until now, you've always had to wait for some special occasion to come along to enjoy these snacks. With these quick and easy recipes for dips and stuff you can eat from the bowl, you'll want to serve munchies more than a few times a year. Now you can dig in when your friends come over or when your family sits down to watch a movie, and still have some left over to stash in your lunchbox. So what are you waiting for? Get munchin'....

Apple Dip

Try this sweet concoction and you'll be eating apples by the bushel!

(Serves 7-10)

You'll need:
4 ounces cream cheese
1/2 teaspoon vanilla
1/3 cup plus 2 teaspoons
   granulated sugar
4 ounces Heath® Bits 'O Brickle®

1. **STOP** With help, use an electric mixer to blend all the ingredients together in a big bowl.

2. Microwave the dip on high for four minutes.

3. Stir the mixture; then put it back in the microwave for one more minute. (**STOP** Be careful when you handle the bowl—it will be HOT!)

4. When the dip is cool, serve it with sliced apples.

Fun Food Fact: There are several hundred different kinds of apples today. In Rome, 2,000 years ago, there were 22 varieties.

Taco Dip

There are so many layers to this delicious dip, scraping
the bottom of the bowl is only half the fun!

(Serves 8)

You'll need:

8 ounces cream cheese

8 ounces sour cream

12 ounces taco sauce

1 cup cheddar or Monterey Jack cheese,
    shredded

1/2 cup chopped tomato

1/2 cup chopped green pepper

1/2 cup black olives, sliced

nacho chips

1. **STOP** With the help of Mom or Dad, use an electric mixer to blend the cream cheese and sour cream until the mixture is very smooth.

2. Pour the cream-cheese mix into the bottom of the serving dish.

3. Spread the taco sauce on top of the cream cheese and sour cream.

4. Sprinkle half of the cheese on top of the taco sauce.

5. Layer the tomatoes on top of the cheese. Next, layer the green peppers on top of the tomatoes. Then, layer the olives on top of the peppers.

6. Sprinkle the rest of the cheese on top. Serve with nacho chips.

Fun Food Fact: Nacho chips are made just like tortillas (see page 110), except they are smaller and contain a few additional spices. The word "nachos" can also mean a popular snack eaten at the movies or football games. Melted cheese, ground beef, refried beans, guacamole, and sour cream are served on top of tortilla chips to make this dish.

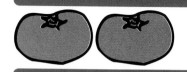

Fresh Tomato Salsa

If you like Mexican food, why not try making homemade salsa? It's much better than that stuff in the jar. It can be served with Mexican dishes or a big bowl of tortilla chips!

(Serves 6)

You'll need:
2 tomatoes, seeded and chopped
1/2 cup chopped onion
1/2 cup chopped green bell pepper
1/2 cup chopped fresh cilantro
2 Tablespoons lemon juice*
1 Tablespoon lime juice
1 jalapeño pepper, seeded and chopped

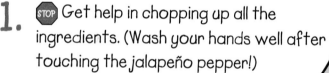

1. **STOP** Get help in chopping up all the ingredients. (Wash your hands well after touching the jalapeño pepper!)

2. In a small bowl, combine all the ingredients. Mix well.

3. Cover and refrigerate about two hours. The salsa can be stored in the fridge for five days.

*1 lemon = 3 Tablespoons lemon juice

Chocolate Popcorn

This popcorn MUST be made in HUGE batches—it disappears fast!

(Serves 15–20)

You'll need:
1/4 cup butter*
1/2 cup chocolate chips
10 cups popped corn

5. Use a spoon to gently separate the popcorn.

1. (STOP) With a grown-up's help, melt the butter and chocolate chips together over medium heat.

2. Put the popped corn into a bowl. Drizzle the chocolate-chip mixture over the popcorn.

3. Make sure you toss it really well, so it coats all the kernels.

4. Put the popcorn in the refrigerator for 20 to 30 minutes.

*1 stick butter = 1/2 cup butter = 8 Tablespoons butter

Fun Food Fact: Over six days in October 1994, students at Beauclerc Elementary School in Jacksonville, Florida, built and filled a HUGE container of popcorn. It was almost 40 feet long, 20 feet 8-1/2 inches wide, and 8 feet high! Now there's something you can't buy at the movie theater!

Pumpkin Seed Toasties

Try this recipe after you finish carving your Halloween jack-o'-lantern.

(Serves 4)

You'll need:
1 pumpkin
2 Tablespoons cooking oil
1 teaspoon salt
1 teaspoon garlic or onion powder
  (if you like)

1. When you clean out your pumpkin, scoop out and save two cups of pumpkin seeds.

2. Wash the seeds and let them dry overnight.

3. Mix the seeds, oil, salt, and garlic or onion powder in a mixing bowl.

4. Spread the seeds on a cookie sheet.

5. **STOP** Bake at 350° for 15 to 20 minutes. (Get help when you use the oven.)

Fun Food Fact: Pumpkins grow on vines and were originally planted by the Native Americans in tropical parts of America. They can be used to make pies, pastries, and pumpkin soup.

Forest Trail Crispies

Here's an easy snack you can make all by yourself and pack in your lunchbox.

(Serves 8)

You'll need:
1 cup peanuts (without the shells)
1 cup M&M's®
1 cup raisins
1 cup Honey-Nut Cheerios®

1. Mix all the ingredients in a large bowl.

2. Serve in the bowl and save some in plastic bags (this way, you can enjoy the snack in your lunchbox all week long).

Fun Food Fact: George Washington Carver thought of hundreds of ways to use peanuts, including in coffee, soap, cheese—and even in *ink!*

After-School Snacks

After a hard day at school, we all need a little pick-me-up. Whether Mom is waiting for you at home, or you take care of yourself after school, it's always good to make sure there are some good things to eat.

In this section, you'll find a bunch of recipes that will have you running home after school even faster than usual! Some of them you can make by yourself when you get home. Others, you and a grown-up can make together. Almost all of them can be made ahead of time so they are ready when you are.

Birdseed Bread

No, it's not really birdseed! But fool your friends and
see if they can tell the difference!

(Makes 10)

You'll need:
1 can refrigerated biscuits
   (10 in a package)
butter
sesame seeds
1 package shelled sunflower seeds

1. Separate the refrigerator biscuits and arrange them on a baking pan.

2. Spread a little butter on top of each biscuit. (Be careful if you are using a knife!)

3. Sprinkle the sesame seeds and the sunflower seeds on top of each biscuit.

4. With your finger or the butter knife, lightly press the seeds into the biscuits, so they don't fall off.

5. **STOP** Get help when you use the oven. Bake the biscuits according to the biscuit package directions. Serve while they are piping hot!

Apple Pie Muffin

This definitely isn't Grandma's apple pie. Think of it as the quick, kids-made version that all your friends will be talking about.

(Makes 1)

You'll need:
1/2 English muffin
butter or margarine
lemon juice
4 apple slices
1/4 teaspoon sugar
1/4 teaspoon cinnamon

1. **STOP** Get help to cut four slices of an apple. (Tell your helper it's okay if he wants to snack on the rest of the apple!) Sprinkle the apple slices with lemon juice to prevent browning.

2. In a small bowl, mix the sugar and cinnamon.

3. Spread a little butter on the muffin. (Be careful if you are using a knife!)

4. Sprinkle some of the cinnamon-and-sugar mixture on top of the muffin.

5. Arrange the apple slices on the muffin, and sprinkle with more of the cinnamon-and-sugar mixture.

6. **STOP** Ask a grown-up to help you toast your muffin in the toaster oven until it begins to turn golden.

7. Let your apple pie muffin cool a bit before you dig in!

Fun Food Fact: Abraham Lincoln LOVED homemade pies. He loved them so much, in fact, that women from his home state of Illinois would mail the president their apple pies.

Yummy Apple Pizzas

Your friends will be amazed at this clever twist on an old favorite.
This sure isn't the same old pizza.

(Makes 10)

You'll need:
1 can of refrigerated biscuits (10 in a can)
2 large apples, peeled and sliced
1/2 cup mild cheddar cheese, grated*
1/4 cup firmly packed brown sugar
1/4 teaspoon cinnamon
2 teaspoons flour
margarine

1. **STOP** Ask a grown-up to preheat the oven to 350°. Lightly grease a baking sheet.

2. In a small bowl, mix together the brown sugar, cinnamon, and flour.

3. Separate the biscuits and place them on the baking sheet. Use your hands to flatten the biscuits.

4. Sprinkle each biscuit with some grated cheddar cheese.

5. Put three apple slices on top of each biscuit.

6. Spoon some of the brown-sugar mixture over the apples; then put a dot of margarine on top.

7. Bake for 25 to 30 minutes. Let the apple pizzas cool before eating.

*4 ounces cheddar or mozzarella = 1 cup

19

 # The Low-Fat Six-Week Muffin

Take a bite out of one of these tasty muffins and you are sure to agree–low-fat doesn't mean low-delicious!

(Makes a whole lot!)

You'll need:
one 15-ounce box of Raisin Bran® cereal
2 cups sugar
5 cups all-purpose flour
5 teaspoons of baking soda
2 teaspoons of salt
1/2 cup vegetable oil
4 eggs, beaten
1 quart low-fat buttermilk

1. In a large bowl, mix the cereal, sugar, flour, baking soda, and salt.

2. Add the oil, eggs, and buttermilk. Mix well.

3. Grease a muffin tin.

4. Fill the muffin-tin cups 1/3 full. STOP With help, bake the muffins at 350° for 15 to 20 minutes.

5. The remaining batter will keep in the refrigerator for six weeks.

Also try:
- adding fruit to the batter just before baking
- frosting the muffins with icing to make cupcakes

Careful Cooking: When cooking with eggs, remember these tips:
- Never use an egg that is cracked.
- Eggs should be stored in the refrigerator, both in the store and when you get home.

FRESH EGGS

Quick Deviled Eggs

This quick appetizer is the perfect snack to make for the next family picnic.

(Makes 1)

You'll need:
1 hard-boiled egg
Thousand Island dressing

1. Peel the hard-boiled egg.

2. **STOP** Cut the egg in half.

3. Scoop out the yolk into a small bowl.

4. Add one teaspoon of Thousand Island dressing and stir.

5. Spoon the mixture back into the egg halves and serve.

Fun Food Fact: Have a question about eggs? There is actually a group of people who can answer it for you. Write to: The American Egg Board, 1460 Renaissance Drive, Suite 301, Park Ridge, IL 60068.

The American Egg Board

Pizza Bites

Do you always end up eating the kind of pizza your kid brother likes? Well, with these personal-size pizzas, you can choose your own toppings to make them just the way you like them.

(Makes 10 little pizzas)

You'll need:
1 can refrigerated biscuits (5 biscuits)
1 cup shredded mozzarella cheese*
1 jar prepared pizza sauce
sliced pepperoni or ground beef,
  chopped onions, chopped peppers,
  and other pizza toppings

1. Spray the bottom of a 9-inch by 13-inch baking pan with nonstick cooking spray.

2. Place the ground beef, onions, peppers, or other toppings in a plastic colander. Put the colander in a microwave-safe bowl. Cook the toppings on high in the microwave until done. (STOP) Ask a grown-up to help you decide when they are all cooked, especially the ground beef or any other meats you may decide to use.

3. (STOP) With help, cut each biscuit in half. Use your hand to flatten each biscuit half. Place each half in the baking pan.

4. Spread pizza sauce over the biscuits. Add the toppings and cheese.

5. (STOP) Ask Mom to bake your pizza bites at 375° for 20 to 30 minutes.

*4 ounces cheddar or mozzarella = 1 cup

Fun Food Fact: The first "modern" pizza was served to Queen Margharita of Italy. It was decorated with the colors of the Italian flag—white cheese, green basil, and red tomatoes.

Rain Forest Mix

This is so easy to make, you can do it all by yourself.
Surprise Mom with a bagful after her hard day at work!

(Serves 3)

You'll need:
1/2 cup peanuts
1/2 cup chocolate chips
1/2 cup cashew nuts
1/2 cup dried banana chips
1/2 cup dried papaya
1/2 cup macadamia nuts
1/2 cup coconut flakes

1. Mix all ingredients together in a large bowl.

2. Eat right away, or store in zippered, plastic bags.

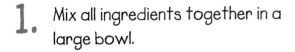

Not-So-Fun Food Fact: The cashews, bananas, papaya, macadamia nuts, and coconut you use in this recipe are all grown in the rain forests of the world. So remember, if the rain forests disappear, so will this recipe. Save the rain forests!

 # Johnny Appleseed Sandwich

Here's a riddle:

When can you make a sandwich without any bread?
When you make this "apple-icious applewich"!

(Makes 1)

You'll need:

2 apple slices
peanut butter
8 raisins

1. **STOP** With help, cut an apple into round slices, about a quarter-inch thick.

2. **STOP** Use a butter knife to spread peanut butter on one of the apple slices.

3. Press the raisins into the peanut butter.

4. Put the other apple slice on top of the peanut butter and raisins. Enjoy your apple sandwich!

Fun Food Fact: To make sandwiches ahead of time, sprinkle the apple slices with lemon juice, so they don't turn brown. When you add lemon juice to the apples, it gets in the way of the reaction between oxygen and apples, so the apples stay their natural color.

Miss Muffet's Delight

If Miss Muffet's curds and whey had been as *yummy* as this treat, she wouldn't have left it behind for some silly spider!

(Serves 6–8)

You'll need:
1 small package orange or lime Jell-O®
one 12-ounce container frozen nondairy
    whipped topping (thawed)
1 pint small-curd cottage cheese
one 6-ounce can crushed pineapple
    (drained)
1 cup miniature marshmallows

1. Spoon the cottage cheese and whipped topping into a large bowl.

2. Sprinkle on dry Jell-O® mix.

3. Stir until well blended.

4. Fold in pineapple and marshmallows.

5. Chill 20 minutes before serving.

Fun Food Fact: When cheese is being made, milk is turned into a solid, except for a pale watery substance that contains sugar and minerals and is separated from milk during the cheese-making process. That watery substance is called whey.

Crunchy Cheese Melts

If you like grilled cheese, you'll love this extraspecial version—
it's got a crunchy kick that will tingle your taste buds!

(Makes 2)

You'll need:
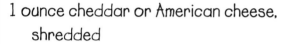

2 rice cakes

1 ounce cheddar or American cheese, shredded

2 tomato slices, as thick as you like them

1 Tablespoon creamy salad dressing

1. **STOP** Ask a grown-up to preheat the oven to 450°.

2. Place the rice cakes on a baking sheet.

3. Put a tomato slice on top of each rice cake.

4. Sprinkle half of the cheese on each tomato slice.

5. **STOP** Bake the rice cakes until the cheese melts, about two minutes.

6. Remove the rice cakes from the oven and top each with a little of the salad dressing.

Careful Cooking: Always keep a list of emergency numbers by the phone so you can call for help if there is an accident.

The Nutty Fruitwich

You may have tasted cream cheese and jelly, and maybe you love peanut butter and jelly, but try this new combination and see if it becomes another favorite.

(Makes 1)

You'll need:
1 Tablespoon creamy peanut butter
1 Tablespoon cream cheese
1 Tablespoon raisins
2 slices bread

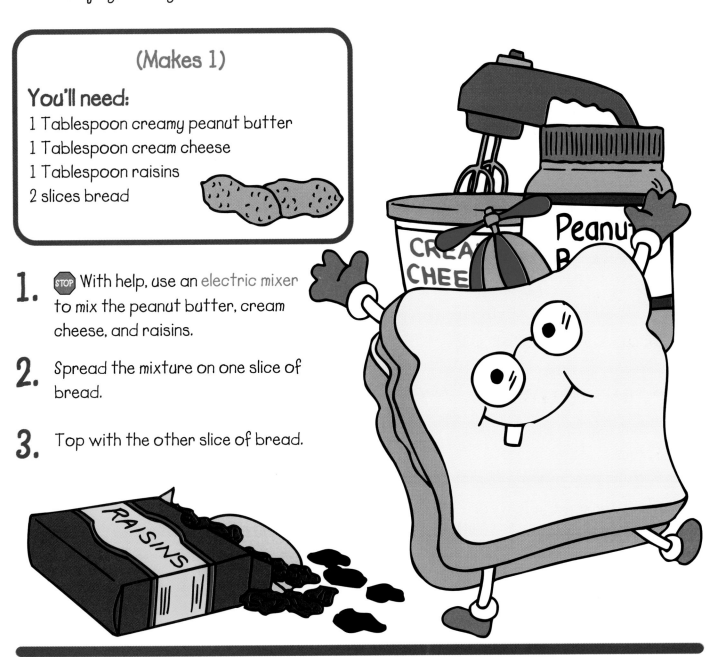

1. **STOP** With help, use an electric mixer to mix the peanut butter, cream cheese, and raisins.

2. Spread the mixture on one slice of bread.

3. Top with the other slice of bread.

Fun Food Fact: The sandwich was invented by John Montagu, the English Earl of Sandwich, in 1762. He was so addicted to gambling, he wouldn't leave the betting table for meals. So his cook prepared a snack for him with a slice of meat between two slices of buttered bread. The snack was an immediate hit in Britain.

Granola Bars

Homemade granola bars are much moister and tastier than anything you'd buy in the store.

(Makes 6)

You'll need:

1 cup plus 2 Tablespoons Bisquick® mix

1/4 cup raisins

3/4 cup uncooked quick-cooking oats

3 Tablespoons firmly packed dark brown sugar

1/2 cup milk

1 egg

1 Tablespoon plus 2 teaspoons margarine, melted*

1 Tablespoon shredded coconut

1. 🛑 Ask a grown-up to preheat the oven to 350°. Spray an 8-inch square baking pan with nonstick cooking spray.

2. In a bowl, combine the Bisquick®, two Tablespoons of raisins, half the oats, and one Tablespoon of sugar. Stir well.

3. Stir in the egg and the milk.

4. Spread this oat mixture into the pan.

5. In another bowl, combine the rest of the raisins, oats, and sugar with the margarine and coconut.

6. Sprinkle this mixture over the oat mix in the pan.

7. 🛑 Bake for 20 to 25 minutes.

8. Set pan on a wire rack until cool.

9. 🛑 Cut into bars. (Ask for help with this part.)

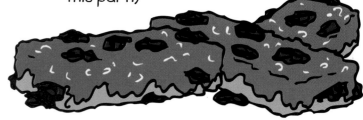

*1 stick margarine = 1/2 cup margarine = 8 Tablespoons margarine

Fun Food Fact: In the late 1860s, a French chemist was the first to make margarine, in a national contest. Napoleon III was looking for a replacement for butter for his army—something that would be cheaper and last longer. Today margarine is made with vegetable oils and skim milk and contains less fat than butter.

REAL Peanut Butter

If you think real peanut butter is what you find in a jar at the store, give this recipe a try. You'll love the rich, nutty flavor.

(Makes about a cup)

You'll need:
1 cup peanuts
1/4 cup peanut oil
crackers or rice cakes

1. Put the peanuts in a blender.

2. Add the oil.

3. (STOP) While an adult is around, blend until the mixture is smooth.

4. Serve on crackers or rice cakes.

Fun Food Fact: Peanuts are known as "ground-nuts" in Africa, where they were first grown. Some farmers also call peanuts "goobers" or "earthnuts" because they grow in underground pods.

Stuff to Slurp

The recipes in this section go way beyond quenching your thirst. Some drinks are thick and creamy and filling—more of a snack than something to sip. They are perfect for an after-school treat or even for dessert. And they're fun to make, too! You get to pour and shake and stir. Some of them are even ready in less than a minute. So what are you waiting for? In 60 seconds, you could be enjoying a long cool slurp of somethin' wonderful!

Surprise Mom with a cup of this spicy tea on a cold wintry afternoon.

(Makes about 3 cups of mix)

You'll need:
1 cup Tang®
1 cup instant tea mix
1 cup granulated sugar
1 teaspoon ground cloves
1 package lemonade mix

---

1. Mix all the ingredients together and store in a jar until you are ready to use it.

2. **STOP** To make a cup of tea, have a grown-up boil the water. Pour the water into a cup. Stir in two to three teaspoonfuls of the tea mix.

3. Stir to mix well.

4. **STOP** Be careful when you take that first sip! This is hot.

Hot Cocoa Mix

This is the creamiest, most chocolatey cocoa ever!

(Serves 1)

You'll need:

3 teaspoons Nestlé® Quik®
2 teaspoons nondairy creamer
1 teaspoon dry milk
1 teaspoon powdered sugar
a few miniature marshmallows (optional)

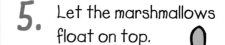

1. Spoon the Nestlé® Quik® into a mug.

2. Add the creamer, dry milk, and powdered sugar to the mug. Stir well.

3. **STOP** With help, boil a pot of water on the stove. (Promise to make your helper a cup of cocoa, too!)

4. Add one cup of boiling water to the mug and stir well.

5. Let the marshmallows float on top.

Fun Food Fact: Until the late 1700s, if you served someone chocolate, you gave them a cup of bitter liquid chocolate with some sugar added. The Aztec Indians of Mexico made the first liquid chocolate from cacao beans. The Spanish army tasted the drink and added sugar to it. They created a new hot drink that the Aztecs called "chocolatl." It is said that Montezuma, the Aztec king, drank 50 cups of chocolate a day!

Fruity Shake

This drink makes a great afternoon snack,
and you don't even need the blender to make it!

(Serves 1)

You'll need:
1 cup cold milk
2 Tablespoons flavored gelatin
(any flavor except lemon)

1. Pour the milk into an airtight container (ask a grown-up what you should use).

2. Add the gelatin.

3. Put the lid on. Make sure it is closed TIGHT!

4. Shake the container for one minute.

5. Pour the mixture into a glass and enjoy!

BANANA STRAWBERRY GELATIN

Root Beer Float

This soda is a classic! Don't be surprised if Mom and Dad get carried away and start sneaking sips from your glass. Just to be safe—make them their own floats!

(Serves 1)

You'll need:
1/2 cup root beer
1 scoop ice cream
1 spoon whipped topping

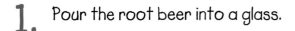

1. Pour the root beer into a glass.

2. Add one scoop of ice cream.

3. Add one spoon of whipped topping.

4. Serve with a straw and a spoon.

Fun Food Fact: Hires[®] Root Beer began as an herb tea. It was invented by Charles Hires, a pharmacist from Philadelphia. In 1876, at the World's Fair, he sold a package of dry herbs, bark, and roots to be brewed at home. By 1886, Hires[®] Root Beer was being sold in bottles.

Pumpkin Smoothies

This shake is like drinking a piece of pumpkin pie! It'll really get you in the mood for trick-or-treating, fall hay rides, and Thanksgiving dinner.

(Serves 1)

You'll need:

1 scoop softened vanilla ice cream
2 Tablespoons cooked pumpkin
1 Tablespoon maple syrup
1/8 teaspoon pumpkin pie spice

1. Place all ingredients in a blender.

2. STOP Ask a grown-up to help you blend the shake. Blend on low until the mixture is smooth.

Careful Cooking: Never wash an electric appliance (like a blender or mixer or toaster) by soaking it in a sink full of water. Unplug the appliance and wash it off with a sponge.

Pineapple Delight Drink

This cool, refreshing drink is perfect when you and
your friends need a summer break.

(Makes a REALLY big bowl)

You'll need:

one 46-ounce can pineapple juice
one 12-ounce can frozen pineapple-
    orange juice concentrate, thawed
one 6-ounce can frozen lemonade
    concentrate, thawed
1/2 gallon pineapple or lemon sherbet,
    softened
flaked coconut (optional)
banana slices or pineapple wedges
    (optional)

3. Sprinkle each serving with coconut.

4. You can also add a banana slice or
pineapple wedge to each cup.

1. In a punch bowl, combine the
pineapple juice, pineapple-orange
juice concentrate, and the lemonade
concentrate.

2. When you are ready to serve
the drink, add the sherbet, one
large spoonful at a time, to the
drink mixture. Stir well.

Creamy Dream Float

Think orange cream pops are just for licking? Well, not anymore!
Now you can drink one, too! Try this ice-cold, creamy shake.

(Serves 1)

You'll need:
2 scoops orange sherbet
3/4 cup milk
whipped topping
coconut, chocolate chips, sprinkles,
    or another topping (optional)

1. Put the sherbet and milk in a blender.

2. (STOP) Blend the mixture for about 30 seconds, until it is smooth.

3. Pour the float into a glass. Top with whipped topping, sprinkles, or other goodies of your choice.

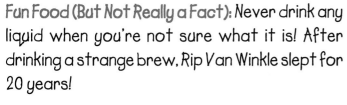

Fun Food (But Not Really a Fact): Never drink any liquid when you're not sure what it is! After drinking a strange brew, Rip Van Winkle slept for 20 years!

Old-Fashioned Lemonade

Sure, there's nothing wrong with lemonade mixes, but with this old-fashioned recipe, you can open the most popular lemonade stand on the block!

(Serves 4)

You'll need:
1/2 cup sugar
1 cup hot water
2 to 3 lemons
2 cups cold water
10 ice cubes

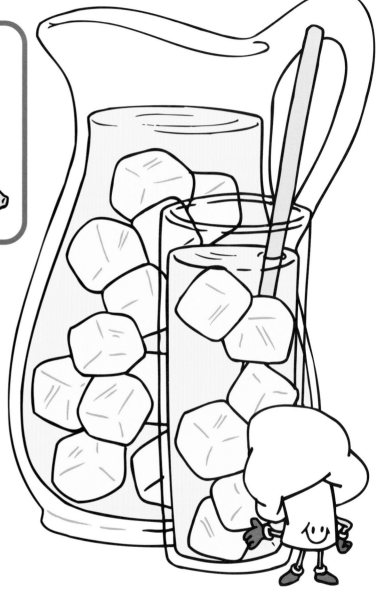

1. Put the sugar in a pitcher and add the hot water. Stir until the sugar is dissolved.

2. (STOP) Ask a grown-up to help cut the lemons in half. Using a juicer, squeeze out the juice. (You should have 1/2 cup.)

3. Mix the lemon juice and the cold water with the sugar water. Add the ice cubes. Stir well.

Fun Food Fact: Not all drinks are as easy to make as lemonade. Coca-Cola® was invented in 1886 by Dr. J. Pemberton in Atlanta, Georgia. He advertised it as "an esteemed brain tonic and intellectual beverage!" There are 15 ingredients in Coke®, and 14 are well-known. The last, a mysterious formula called "7x," is top secret.

Saturday Afternoon Treats

A great way to spend a Saturday afternoon is helping Mom in the kitchen—especially if she's making some *yummy stuff for you!* You can use this time to practice your cooking skills, experiment with new recipes, or whip up a batch of old favorites.

Spend a fall afternoon raking leaves and then mixing up a warm loaf of bread, or savor a hot August day by concocting your own tub of ice cream. Whether you want something creamy, crunchy, sweet, or zesty, you'll find the perfect recipe to share with Mom or Dad.

Noodle Nests

These sweet, crunchy treats take almost no time to make. They are a great way to celebrate Easter or springtime, but you can find an excuse to make them almost any time of the year.

(Makes about 16)

You'll need:
1 can chocolate frosting
4 cups thin chow mein noodles
jelly beans

1. STOP Ask a grown-up to heat the frosting in a pot over low heat. Stir it until it becomes a liquid.

2. Remove the frosting from the stove. Stir in the noodles.

3. Drop by 1/4 cupfuls onto a cookie sheet.

4. Press with the back of a spoon to form nests.

5. Add jelly beans. Let set until firm.

Careful Cooking: If a pot or pan catches fire, DO NOT throw water on it. Cover it with a lid and it will go out on its own.

Snowball Treats

Just like real snowballs, these scrumptious treats won't be around for long!

(Makes 35)

You'll need:

6 cups crisp rice cereal

1/4 cup butter or margarine*

1 package marshmallows (10 ounces)

2 cups powdered sugar

1. Put the powdered sugar inside a resealable plastic bag.

2. (STOP) Get help to melt the butter in a large pan over low heat.

3. Add the marshmallows. Stir constantly until they are all melted.

4. Remove the pot from the stove.

5. Stir in the cereal, and mix until the cereal is well coated. Allow the mixture to cool.

6. When the mixture is cool enough to handle, shape into small balls.

7. Drop a few balls into the bag of sugar. Gently shake until the balls are dusted with powdered sugar.

8. Repeat for the rest of the snowballs.

*1 stick butter = 1/2 cup butter = 8 Tablespoons butter

Fun Food Fact: Marshmallows were originally made from the root of North Africa's marsh mallow plant, which grows in marshes and other swampy areas. Today, marshmallows are made from corn syrup, sugar, and gelatin.

Crunchy Cacti

Our sweet cactus crunchies are no mirage!

(Makes 15 to 20)

You'll need:

one 12-ounce package of butterscotch chips

2 Tablespoons peanut butter

green food coloring

one 6-ounce can chow mein noodles

6. When the mixture is cool enough to touch, shape golf ball-size portions into cactus shapes.

7. Let the cacti harden. Then you are ready to chow down!

1. [STOP] With help, melt the chips over low heat, stirring occasionally.

2. Stir in peanut butter.

3. Stir in the green food coloring. Add a little at a time, until it's the shade of green you want.

4. Add the chow mein noodles. Stir until well coated.

5. Remove the mixture from the stovetop to cool.

Chef's Secret: To easily melt chocolate, butterscotch, and other morsels, try placing the chips in a glass measuring cup and microwave on high for 45 seconds to 1 minute. Stir until smooth.

Russian Tea Cakes

Try this recipe and you'll be saying
"Da! Kharasho!" (dah! KHAAH raah show!)—Yes! Good!

(Makes a bunch)

You'll need:
1 cup butter, softened*
1/2 cup powdered sugar
1 teaspoon vanilla
2-1/4 cups all-purpose flour
1/4 teaspoon salt
3/4 cup finely chopped nuts**
powdered sugar for dusting

1. (STOP) Ask a grown-up to preheat the oven to 400˚.

2. Mix butter, powdered sugar, and vanilla in a bowl.

3. Mix in flour, salt, and nuts until the dough holds together.

4. Shape the dough into one-inch balls.

5. Place each ball, about one inch apart, on an ungreased cookie sheet.

6. (STOP) With help, bake until set, but don't let the cookies get brown—about 10 to 12 minutes.

7. Roll the tea cakes in powdered sugar before they cool.

*1 stick butter = 1/2 cup butter = 8 Tablespoons butter
**4 ounces nuts = 1 cup chopped nuts

Chef's Secret: Do not use margarine in recipes unless the recipe calls for it. Margarine has less fat than butter and will make your recipes come out drier.

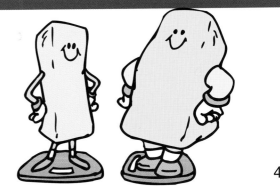

Blooming Biscuits

These pretty biscuits are quick and easy to make.
They are a perfect way to surprise Mom on Mother's Day.

(Makes 10)

You'll need:
1 package of refrigerator biscuits
   (10 in a package)
a jar of jam or jelly

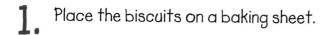

1. Place the biscuits on a baking sheet.

2. **STOP** With help, cut around the edges of each biscuit, to shape it into a flower with four petals. (See below.)

3. Use your thumb to press down in the center of each biscuit flower.

4. **STOP** Bake the biscuits according to the directions on the biscuit package.

5. Remove from the oven. Let the biscuits cool for a few minutes.

6. Spoon a little jam into the center of each biscuit flower.

Pumpkin Nut Bread

This sweet, nutty bread is great to make around the holidays.
Make a few extra to wrap up for Grandma and Grandpa.

(Makes 4 mini loaves)

You'll need:
1 teaspoon baking soda
1/3 cup water
1-1/2 cups sugar
1/2 teaspoon salt
1 teaspoon cinnamon
1/2 teaspoon nutmeg
2 eggs, beaten separately
1/2 cup oil
1 cup canned pumpkin
1-3/4 cups sifted flour
1/2 cup raisins
1/4 cup chopped walnuts

1. **STOP** Ask a grown-up to preheat the oven to 350°. Grease four mini loaf pans.

2. In a small bowl, dissolve the baking soda in the water. Set aside.

3. In a large bowl, combine the sugar, salt, cinnamon, and nutmeg.

4. Add the eggs one at a time. Then add the oil. Beat well after each addition.

5. Stir in the pumpkin and the baking soda solution.

6. First add half the flour. Beat well. Now add the rest of the flour. Beat well again.

7. Stir in the raisins and nuts.

8. Spoon the batter into the mini loaf pans.

9. Bake for 35 to 40 minutes.

Fun Food Fact: Nutmeg is made by grating the kernel of the fruit that comes from a tropical tree, which grows about 65 feet tall.

Indian Fry Bread

This is a harvesttime treat made by Native Americans.
It's a great snack for a chilly October or November day.

You'll need:
2-1/2 cups flour
1/4 teaspoon salt
1 teaspoon baking powder
3/4 cup water
1/4 cup milk
cinnamon, sugar, or honey

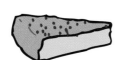

1. In a large bowl, mix together the flour, salt, and baking powder.

2. Stir the water and milk into the flour mixture.

3. **STOP** With help, pour the batter into a pan and fry until golden.

4. Sprinkle with cinnamon, sugar, or honey.

Fun Food Fact: Boiled eel, lobster, roasted pigeon, and stuffed cod were served by the colonists at the first Thanksgiving. It was the Native Americans who brought our now-traditional dishes of turkey, pumpkins, sweet potatoes, and cranberry sauce.

Ice Cream in a Can

Ice cream IN A CAN??? It sounds strange,
but here is an easy way to make your own frozen treats at home.

(Serves 4)

You'll need:
1 egg
1/2 cup sugar
1 Tablespoon vanilla instant pudding mix
1 cup milk
1 cup half-and-half (cream)
dash of vanilla
rock salt
crushed ice

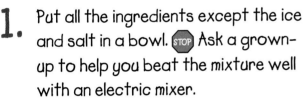

1. Put all the ingredients except the ice and salt in a bowl. (STOP) Ask a grown-up to help you beat the mixture well with an electric mixer.

2. Pour the mixture into a one-pound coffee can.

3. Cover with Saran Wrap®. Then put on the plastic lid.

4. Place the container in a three-pound coffee can.

5. Add the ice and salt around the smaller can. Cover with the plastic lid.

6. Roll the can on the floor for about 20 minutes.

7. If the center of the ice cream is still soft, place the containers in a freezer until the ice cream hardens.

Nutty Putty

You can sculpt, mold, and play with this dough before you eat it!

(Makes 7–10 portions)

You'll need:
1-3/4 cups peanut butter
2 cups powdered sugar
1-3/4 cups corn syrup or honey
2 cups powdered milk
chocolate chips

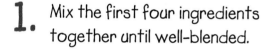

1. Mix the first four ingredients together until well-blended.

2. Mold and shape the dough on waxed paper.

3. Use chocolate chips as decorations on your creations.

4. Eat 'em up!

Dried Apple Rings

This harvest treat was enjoyed by the early settlers.

(How much it makes depends on how many apples you cut)

You'll need:

apples
sunshine

1. **STOP** Get help peeling the apples.

2. **STOP** With Mom's help, slice the apples into thin rings. Cut out the cores.

3. Place the apples between two pieces of window screen. Set the apples outside in a hot, sunny place.

4. Turn and rearrange the apples as they are drying (it takes about one to two weeks).

5. When apples are dried, serve as they are, or make apple turnovers with them.

Apple Turnovers

You'll need:

dried apple rings
1 package refrigerator biscuits
sugar
cinnamon
vegetable oil

1. **STOP** Ask an adult to cook the dried apples in water until tender. Add sugar and cinnamon to taste.

2. To make a turnover, flatten a refrigerator biscuit with your hand.

3. Spoon the apples onto half of the circle of dough.

4. Fold over the other half and seal the edges.

5. **STOP** Ask an adult to fry the biscuits in oil on top of the stove.

6. Drain the turnovers on paper towels. Serve when they are cool.

Popcorn Balls

Make these for your family, your classmates, or even for trick-or-treaters.

(Serves a crowd)

You'll need:

1 cup granulated sugar or
    firmly packed brown sugar
1/3 cup light or dark corn syrup
1/3 cup water
1/4 cup butter or margarine*
1/2 teaspoon salt
1 teaspoon vanilla
2 quarts popped popcorn

1. STOP Warm the popcorn in a 250° oven.

2. In a two-quart saucepan, stir together sugar, corn syrup, water, butter, and salt.

3. STOP With help, cook the sugar mixture over medium heat. Stir constantly until it comes to a boil.

4. STOP Have a grown-up attach a candy thermometer to the pan.

5. STOP Heat without stirring until mixture reaches 270°. A small amount dropped in very cold water will separate into hard, but not brittle, threads.

6. Remove the saucepan from the stove. Add vanilla and stir only enough to mix with the hot syrup.

7. Pour syrup slowly over popped corn, mixing it with a fork. Continue to toss and mix to cover the popcorn evenly.

8. When the mixture is cool enough to handle but still warm, shape as desired.

*1 stick butter = 1/2 cup butter = 8 Tablespoons butter

Tip: To make popcorn lollipops, press the slightly cooled mixture into muffin tins. Insert a Popsicle® stick into each. Gently remove the lollipops from pans. Place on waxed paper until set.

Careful Cooking: Do not wear long or baggy sleeves and long, loose hair when you are cooking. Keep these clear of the burners on the stove and all electric appliances.

 # Caramel Popcorn Balls

When these popcorn balls are cool, wrap them in colored plastic wrap and hang them on your Christmas tree!

(Makes 9)

You'll need:
2-1/2 quarts popped popcorn
one 14-ounce package light caramels
1/4 cup light corn syrup
2 Tablespoons water

1. **STOP** Keep popcorn warm in a 250° oven.

2. **STOP** With help, melt caramels in the top of a double boiler.

3. Add corn syrup and water. Mix until smooth.

4. Slowly pour over popcorn in large bowl or pan. Mix well.

5. When cool enough to handle, but still warm, shape into 2-1/2 inch balls.

Fun Food Fact: Milton Snavely Hershey originally sold caramels for a living, before he began making chocolate bars.

Snow Cones

These frozen confections are quick and easy and fun for a hot, summer day right in your own backyard (or kitchen).

(The number of snow cones this recipe makes depends on how much ice you use)

You'll need:
fruit-flavored Jell-O® mix
clean, crushed ice

1. Mix the Jell-O® according to package directions.

2. Pack the ice into paper cups.

3. Drizzle the Jell-O® syrup over the ice.

4. Enjoy!

Fun Food Fact: One night in 1905, Frank Epperson of San Francisco left a mixing stick in a glass of lemonade by his windowsill. The next day, the lemonade was frozen into the "first ice lollipop." The treat was first called the "epsicle," but later became the Popsicle®.

Caramel Crispy Treats

This treat combines some of your favorite snacks all at once!

(Makes 9)

You'll need:
one 14-ounce package vanilla caramels
(about 50 pieces)
1/4 cup milk
4 cups unsweetened crispy rice cereal
1 cup salted peanuts

1. **Grease** an 8-inch square baking pan.

2. Place the caramels and milk in a large microwaveable dish. **STOP** Microwave on high for one minute. Stir well. Microwave one more minute on high. Stir again. Repeat this step until the caramels are completely melted.

3. Add cereal and peanuts. Stir well.

4. Spread cereal mixture evenly in pan.

5. Allow to set for one hour or until firm.

6. Cut into two-inch squares.

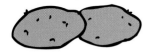 # Stuffed Potato Skins

Better make plenty of these! Kids love 'em, dads devour them!

(Makes 8)

You'll need:
4 baking potatoes
cheddar cheese, shredded
bacon bits
sour cream, salsa, guacamole

1. STOP Ask a grown-up to preheat the oven to 375°.

2. Wash the potatoes. Poke a few holes in each with a fork.

3. STOP Bake in the oven for one hour. Do not turn off the oven when you take them out.

4. Let them cool until you can hold them.

5. STOP With help, cut the baked potatoes in half and scoop out most of the potato. (See below to find out what to do with the potato leftovers.)

6. Sprinkle cheddar cheese and bacon bits on each skin. Stuff in as much as you like.

7. Put the skins on a baking sheet. STOP Put the skins back in the oven. Bake about 10 minutes, or until cheese is melted and bubbly.

8. Serve the skins with sour cream, salsa, or guacamole.

Tip: What to do with the leftover potatoes? Mash them with a mixer or potato masher. Add butter, a little milk, and salt and pepper, and you've got old-fashioned mashed potatoes! You can also mix them with a little garlic powder and mozzarella cheese, form them into patties, and fry them in a pan. Yummy!!!!

Fun Food Fact: Potatoes were grown for a long time by the Indians in Chile and Peru. In 1537, the Spanish army discovered loads of potatoes stored in the Incan city of Sorocata. In 1554, Pizarro brought the potato to Spain. Its popularity spread throughout Europe in the years to follow.

Microwave S'mores

This favorite campfire treat has been around since
Grandma and Grandpa were little campers!

You'll need:
graham crackers
chocolate bars
marshmallows

5. STOP Microwave on high for 15 seconds or until the marshmallow is mushy and the chocolate is melted.

1. Put a piece of a chocolate bar on top of a graham cracker.

2. Place a marshmallow on top of the piece of chocolate.

3. Top off the whole thing with another graham cracker.

4. Wrap the marshmallow sandwich in a paper towel.

Fun Food Fact: Percy Le Baron Spencer, an American scientist, discovered the microwave oven by accident in 1946. He was studying the emission of short-wave electromagnetic energy, when he noticed the microwaves had melted a piece of candy in his pocket. Microwave ovens cook food by making the molecules in a food item vibrate, creating heat. The first microwave oven was marketed in 1947.

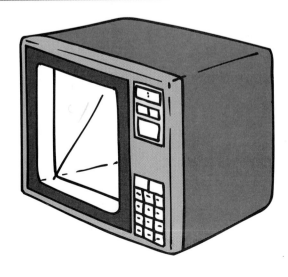

Baked Caramel Apples

Here's a simple version of a favorite carnival treat.

(Serves 6)

You'll need:
3 apples
6 caramel candies (unwrapped)
2 Tablespoons butter*
1/2 cup water

1. **STOP** With help, cut the apples in half and remove the cores.

2. Put one dot of butter and one caramel in each apple half.

3. Grease a small baking dish.

4. Place the apples and 1/2 cup water in the dish.

5. **STOP** Bake the apples for about 15 minutes at 475°.

6. Cool before eating.

*1 stick butter = 1/2 cup butter = 8 Tablespoons butter

Fun Food Fact: A man in Indianapolis picked 15,830 pounds of apples in only eight hours in September 1980.

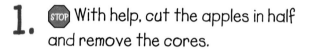

Popcorn and Peanut Yummy

Making your own candy is a snap with this recipe!

(Makes about 2 dozen)

You'll need:
1 cup chocolate chips
1 cup popcorn
1 cup peanuts

1. **STOP** With help, melt the chocolate chips in a pan on the stovetop.

2. Add the popcorn and nuts.

3. Stir well until they are coated.

4. Drop the mixture, using a teaspoon, onto waxed paper.

5. Let the candy set.

Baked Goodies

There's something about the smell of warm baked goodies right out of the oven! Just think of all the "yummylicious" things that go into cookies and cakes: cinnamon, jam, brown sugar, cherries, chocolate chips....Mmmm!!! So the next time you find yourself scraping the bottom of the cookie jar, don't reach for another box of store-bought cookies! Whip up a batch of one of our tasty treats and share them with Mom and Dad (you're never too grown up for a nice big brownie!).

Friendship Wreath Cake

This delicious cake is like a giant cinnamon roll. Pull off pieces to share with friends.

(Makes 8–10 slices)

You'll need:
2 cans refrigerated biscuits
1 stick melted butter
1 cup sugar
2 teaspoons cinnamon

1. Separate the biscuits. **STOP** Get help when you cut each one into four pieces.

2. Roll each piece of dough into a ball.

3. Mix together the sugar and cinnamon.

4. Drop about a third of the balls of dough into a greased Bundt pan so that they are evenly distributed.

5. Sprinkle one third of the cinnamon and sugar over the dough balls.

6. Drop half of the remaining dough balls evenly into the Bundt pan.

7. Sprinkle half of the remaining sugar and cinnamon mixture over them.

8. Drop the rest of the dough balls into the pan.

9. Sprinkle the rest of the cinnamon and sugar mixture on top.

10. Pour the melted butter over the top of the dough balls.

11. **STOP** Bake the cake at 350° for 30 to 35 minutes.

12. Let the cake cool a bit before turning it upside down.

Fun Food Fact: The world's oldest cake is on display at the Alimentarium Food Museum in Vevey, Switzerland. The cake was sealed and "vacuum-packed" in the grave of an ancient Egyptian around 2200 B.C.! It has sesame seeds on top and honey inside.

Easy Cherry Tarts

We cannot tell a lie—you can bake these tarts quicker than
you can chop down a cherry tree! *

(Makes 8 –10)

You'll need:

1 package refrigerator biscuits
   (8 to 10 biscuits)
1 can cherry pie filling

1. Separate the biscuits and place them on a baking sheet.

2. Use your hand to flatten each biscuit.

3. Put a spoonful of cherry pie filling in the center of each flattened biscuit.

4. Fold the biscuit in half and press the edges together with a fork.

5. 🛑 With help, bake the tarts according to the directions on the biscuit package.

*Legends say that George Washington once chopped down a cherry tree when he was a little boy. When his father asked who had done it, he said, "I cannot tell a lie. I did it."

Make home-baked cookies in half the time.

(Makes 1 pan)

You'll need:

1 box white or yellow cake mix
2 eggs
one 6-ounce bag chocolate chips
1 stick margarine, melted
1/2 cup chopped pecans (optional)

1. Mix all the ingredients in a bowl.

2. Spread the mixture in a 9-inch by 13-inch baking pan.

3. **STOP** Ask a grown-up to bake the cake at 350° for 30 minutes.

4. Cool and cut into squares.

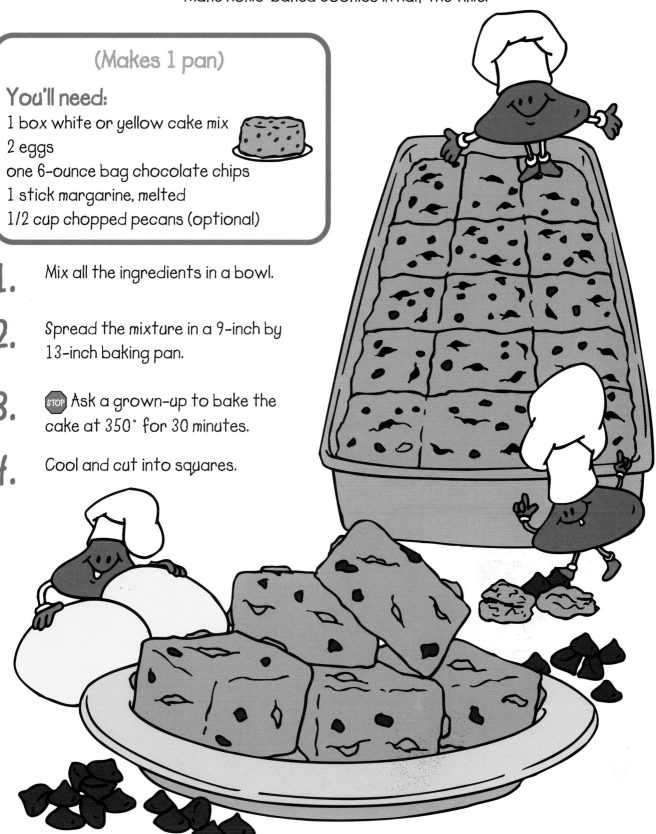

Cherry Crisp

The next time Mom or Dad cooks over a hot grill, whip up this easy summer dessert as a special surprise.

(Serves 6–8)

You'll need:
2 cans cherry pie filling
1/2 cup margarine, melted*
1 yellow cake mix

1. Pour the pie filling into a 9-inch square pan (ask for help when you open the cans).

2. Mix the cake mix with the melted margarine.

3. Crumble the cake mix over the pie filling.

4. **STOP** Bake the crisp at 350˚ for 30 minutes.

*1 stick margarine = 1/2 cup margarine = 8 Tablespoons margarine

Careful Cooking: Always use pot holders when you touch hot pots, pans, and dishes, whether they are coming off the stovetop, from the oven, or out of the microwave.

Individual Apple Crisp

Surprise Mom with this easy microwave dessert and you'll be the apple of her eye!

(Makes 1)

You'll need:
1 apple, peeled and sliced
1 Tablespoon raisins (optional)
1/2 cup granola
1 teaspoon cinnamon
vanilla ice cream

1. Place the cinnamon and apple pieces in a resealable plastic bag. Toss to coat the apple pieces.

2. Put the coated apple pieces in a microwave-safe dish. **STOP** Cook three minutes. Test the apples to see if they have softened. Cook another three minutes and test again until they are soft.

3. Remove the apple pieces from the microwave. Stir in the granola and raisins.

4. Top with ice cream.

Pumpkin Muffins

These muffins are perfect for breakfast, as lunchbox desserts, and as after-school munchies.

(Makes 12 large muffins)

You'll need:

1 egg
3/4 cup milk
2 Tablespoons oil
1/2 cup cooked pumpkin
1/2 cup sugar
3/4 teaspoon pumpkin pie spice
2 cups biscuit mix

1. Mix the egg, milk, oil, and cooked pumpkin in a bowl.

2. Add the sugar, pumpkin pie spice, and biscuit mix.

3. Mix all the ingredients until they are well blended. Pour into greased or paper-lined muffin cups.

4. STOP With help, bake your muffins at 350˚ for 25 minutes.

Fun Food Fact: The largest varieties of pumpkins can grow to weigh over 100 pounds each!

Applesauce Cookies

Serve these cookies with apple cider and you have the
perfect end to a winter's day.

(Makes 6 dozen)

You'll need:
1 box of spice cake mix
   (enough for a two-layer cake)
1 cup raisins
1/2 cup oil
1/2 cup applesauce
1 egg

1. In a large bowl, combine all the ingredients. Mix well.

2. Drop teaspoonfuls two inches apart on an ungreased cookie sheet.

3. STOP With help, bake your cookies at 350° for 12 to 15 minutes.

Chef's Secret: If your parents are health-conscious, here's a trick to cut down on the fat and calories in cakes and cookies. If a recipe calls for oil, use only 1/4 of the amount that it says and use applesauce for the rest. For example, if the recipe says 1 cup of oil, use 1/4 cup of oil and 3/4 cup of applesauce. The applesauce leaves the baked goods moist and does not change the flavor at all!

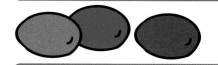 # Robin's Nest

Celebrate spring with these edible birds' nests!

(Makes 12)

You'll need:
4 large shredded wheat biscuits
1/2 cup coconut
2 Tablespoons brown sugar
1/2 cup margarine, melted*
jelly beans

1. Crumble the shredded wheat in a bowl.

2. *Stir* in the coconut, sugar, and melted margarine. Mix well.

3. Press the shredded wheat mixture into muffin-tin cups lined with foil.

4. 🛑 With help, bake the nests at 350° for ten minutes.

5. When the nests have cooled, remove them from the muffin cups. Fill with jelly beans.

*1 stick margarine = 1/2 cup margarine = 8 Tablespoons margarine

Fun Food Fact: Before 1967, it was illegal to sell yellow margarine in Wisconsin. Because that state produces butter and other dairy products, it didn't want anything to replace butter.

Fall Haystacks

These sweet and crunchy candies are perfect Halloween party snacks.

(Servings vary depending on how many ounces of chips and chow mein noodles are used)

You'll need:
2 packages peanut butter chips*
1 large package chow mein noodles
1 small can cocktail peanuts

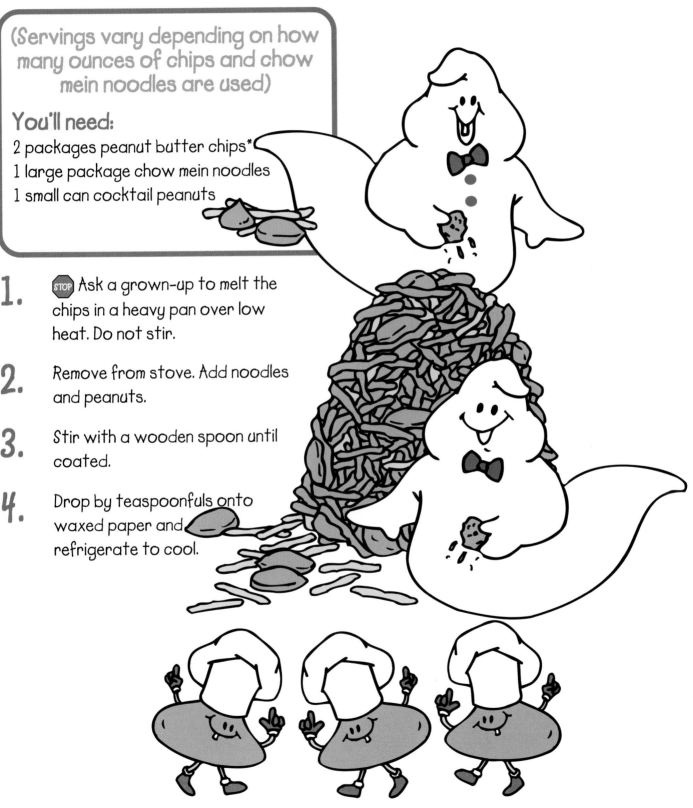

1. STOP Ask a grown-up to melt the chips in a heavy pan over low heat. Do not stir.

2. Remove from stove. Add noodles and peanuts.

3. Stir with a wooden spoon until coated.

4. Drop by teaspoonfuls onto waxed paper and refrigerate to cool.

*Butterscotch and chocolate chips may be substituted.

Goosters

Goosters are chewy, gooey cookies that are fun and sticky to eat.
Don't forget the milk!

(Makes 1 pan)

You'll need:
1 egg
2/3 cup packed brown sugar
1/3 cup maple syrup
1/2 cup flour
1/4 teaspoon salt
1/4 teaspoon baking soda
3/4 cup chopped walnuts
1/4 cup chopped dates

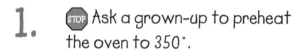

6. **Grease** an 8-inch square pan. Pour the mix into the pan.

7. (STOP) With help, bake the cookies at 350° for 25 minutes.

8. Let them cool a bit (as they cool, they will harden). Cut into small squares.

1. (STOP) Ask a grown-up to preheat the oven to 350°.

2. Use a wire **whisk** to beat the egg. Mix in the brown sugar and maple syrup.

3. In a second bowl combine the flour, salt, and baking soda.

4. Blend the two mixtures together.

5. Mix in the walnuts and dates.

Careful Cooking: Wash your hands with hot, soapy water after handling eggs.

Special Banana Bread

This banana bread has a special burst of flavor inside!

(Makes 1 loaf)

You'll need:

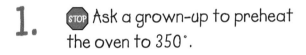

3 bananas
1/4 cup honey
3/4 cup sugar
3 Tablespoons butter, softened and at
    room temperature*
2 eggs
1/2 teaspoon vanilla extract
2 cups flour
1/2 teaspoon salt
1/2 teaspoon baking soda
1 teaspoon baking powder
1/2 cup strawberry jam, raspberry jam,
    or orange marmalade

1. STOP Ask a grown-up to preheat the oven to 350°.

2. Combine flour, salt, baking powder, and baking soda.

3. In a separate bowl, mash the bananas with a potato masher.

4. Mix the honey, sugar, butter, eggs, and vanilla with the bananas.

5. Blend the flour mix and the banana mix together.

6. Grease a loaf pan. Pour two-thirds of the batter into the pan.

7. Spread a layer of the jam over the batter. Pour the rest of the batter on top.

8. STOP Bake the bread at 350° for 55 minutes.

*1 stick butter = 1/2 cup butter = 8 Tablespoons butter

Chocolate Chip Cookies

No cookbook is complete without a recipe for this favorite cookie.

(Makes 2 dozen)

You'll need:

1/2 stick butter or margarine, softened*
1/3 cup firmly packed brown sugar
1/4 cup granulated sugar
3/4 teaspoon vanilla extract
1 egg white
1-1/2 cups all-purpose flour
3/4 teaspoon baking soda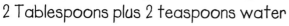
2 Tablespoons plus 2 teaspoons water
1/2 cup semisweet chocolate morsels

1. (STOP) Ask an adult to preheat the oven to 350°.

2. Spray two nonstick baking sheets with nonstick cooking spray.

3. (STOP) With help, beat the butter, both sugars, and the vanilla on medium speed until the mixture gets fluffy. Beat in the egg white.

4. In another bowl, combine the flour and baking soda. Mix well.

5. (STOP) Switch the mixer speed to low. Pour a little of the flour mix into the butter mix and blend. Then pour in a little water. Continue pouring in a little bit of the flour and water and mixing well.

6. Stir in the chocolate morsels.

7. Use a teaspoon to drop dough onto the baking sheets. Keep the spoons of dough about an inch apart.

8. (STOP) Bake the cookies until they are lightly golden (about 10 to 12 minutes).

9. Place the baking sheets on a wire rack to cool till just warm.

10. Use a spatula to move the cookies off the baking sheets and set them out on the **wire rack**. Let them cool completely.

*1 stick butter = 1/2 cup butter = 8 Tablespoons butter

Tip: Save time! Make cookie bars in a 9-inch square baking pan. Spray the pan with nonstick cooking spray. Press the dough into the pan. Bake about 20 minutes until golden. Let the pan cool completely. Then cut into squares.

Best Brownies

Everyone loves brownies. So make a lot, and serve them hot!

(Makes 16 brownie squares)

You'll need:

2/3 cup unsweetened cocoa powder
1/2 cup all-purpose flour
1/2 teaspoon baking powder
1/4 teaspoon salt
1/2 cup vegetable oil
1/2 cup firmly packed light brown sugar
1/2 cup granulated sugar
4 egg whites
1 teaspoon vanilla extract

1. 🛑 Ask a grown-up to preheat the oven to 350˚.

2. Spray an 8-inch square baking pan with nonstick cooking spray.

3. In a bowl, combine the cocoa, flour, baking powder, and salt.

4. In another bowl, **whisk** together oil, both sugars, egg whites, and vanilla. Blend well.

5. Stir the cocoa mixture into the sugar mixture. Pour the brownie mix into the pan.

6. 🛑 Bake the brownies for about 25 minutes. The brownies are done when you can stick a toothpick in the center, pull it out, and none of the mix sticks to it.

7. Place pan on a **wire rack**. Let brownies cool completely. With help, cut your brownies into squares. (Or serve your brownies warm with whipped cream.)

Tip: For extraspecial brownies, try this! When the brownies are done, place them on a wire rack to cool. After ten minutes, take 1-1/2 cups of mini marshmallows and sprinkle them on the brownies. Drizzle some chocolate syrup over the top. Put the pan back in the oven for about three minutes. Let the pan cool completely on a wire rack. WIth help, cut your brownies into squares.

Chef's Secret: For a quick cleanup after making brownies, line the brownie pan with waxed paper before you pour in the batter. When the brownies finish cooling, just lift them out of the pan by pulling up the edges of the waxed paper.

Look Ma! No Oven!

Getting tired of asking Mom to help you with the stove for EVERY recipe? It's still a good idea to ask a grown-up to help if you need to use knives, the oven, or a mixer. But are you ready to do some pouring, mixing, and combining all by yourself? That's why we've included the following recipes. None of these recipes have to be baked. So impress your friends and family with these quick-to-fix snacks.

# No-Bake Chocolate Cookies

Can you make cookies without baking them? Well, try this nutty recipe!

(Makes 50 small cookies)

You'll need:
3 cups uncooked oatmeal
1/2 cup shredded coconut
1/2 cup chopped nuts*
1/2 cup cocoa
1/2 cup evaporated milk
1/2 cup butter or margarine**
2 cups sugar
1/2 teaspoon vanilla

1. In a large bowl, mix together oatmeal, coconut, and nuts. Set aside.

2. In a saucepan, combine cocoa, evaporated milk, butter, and sugar.

3. STOP Ask a grown-up to cook the cocoa mixture over medium heat. Stir occasionally, until it reaches a full boil. Boil for one minute.

4. Remove from the stovetop and add vanilla.

5. Pour mixture over the dry ingredients.

6. Using a fork, stir the mixture until the dry ingredients are well-coated.

7. Drop by teaspoonfuls onto waxed paper. (Work quickly, since the mixture will harden rapidly.) Let cookies stand until firm.

*4 ounces nuts = 1 cup chopped nuts
**1 stick butter = 1/2 cup butter = 8 Tablespoons butter

Fun Food Fact: In some parts of Italy, the walnut tree is called the witches' tree. And in the past, the ancient Romans considered the walnut the nut of the gods, and the Greeks dedicated their walnuts to Artemis, their goddess of the moon.

Oatmeal Crunchies

Your grandmother will think these cookies took hours to make!

(Makes 4 dozen cookies)

You'll need:
1/2 cup butter*
1/2 cup milk
2 cups sugar
1/4 cup cocoa
1/2 cup peanut butter
1-1/2 teaspoons vanilla
3-1/4 cups uncooked oatmeal

1. **STOP** Get help to heat the butter and milk.

2. Add the sugar and cocoa. **STOP** Boil the mixture for five minutes.

3. Add peanut butter, vanilla, and uncooked oats. Stir until well blended.

4. Drop the mixture by teaspoons onto waxed paper.

5. Let the cookies stand for 30 minutes or until firm.

*1 stick butter = 1/2 cup butter = 8 Tablespoons

Careful Cooking: When you use the stovetop, make sure pot handles don't stick out from the stove. Someone could walk by, bump into one, and get a bad burn.

74

Wiggle Worm Pie

Look for worms in this dessert you can make all by yourself.

(Serves 1)

You'll need:
1 foil cupcake wrapper (NOT a paper muffin-tin liner)
3 chocolate cookies
1 small box of instant chocolate pudding
1 Gummy Worm®

1. Place the cookies in a plastic bag. Crush them into crumbs.

2. Prepare the chocolate pudding according to package directions.

3. Scoop a little of the cookie crumbs into a foil cupcake wrapper.

4. Lay the Gummy Worm® on top.

5. Cover the Gummy Worm® with most of the cookie crumbs.

6. Spoon some of the chocolate pudding into the foil cupcake wrapper, on top of the crumbs.

7. Sprinkle the rest of the cookie crumbs on top.

Coconut Delights

Here's a quick and easy after-school snack to make when friends come over.

(Makes enough to use all the vanilla wafers)

You'll need:

one 16-ounce box vanilla wafers
one 10-1/2-ounce bag
    miniature marshmallows
one 12-ounce bag semisweet
    chocolate chips
1 stick margarine
2 cups coconut
green food coloring
miniature jelly beans or candy eggs

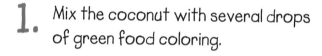

1. Mix the coconut with several drops of green food coloring.

2. Melt the marshmallows, chocolate chips, and margarine in a microwave.

3. Lay the vanilla wafers out on a tray or waxed paper.

4. Spread the chocolate mixture on the top of each wafer.

5. Sprinkle the coconut on top of the chocolate.

6. Place a few jelly beans on each wafer.

Chef's Secret: If you need miniature marshmallows for a recipe and you have only the big ones, use scissors (ask for help!) to cut them into little pieces. Spray the scissors with nonstick cooking spray so that the marshmallows will not stick to them.

Candy Angel Cake

Surprise Mom! Have this quick and easy dessert cake ready and waiting when she gets home from work.

(Makes 10–12 Servings)

You'll need:
one 12-ounce angel food cake
one 5-ounce box instant vanilla pudding
one 12-ounce container Cool Whip®
3 large Heath® or Skör® candy bars, crushed

1. Shred the angel food cake (with your fingers) in a 9-inch by 13-inch pan.

2. Mix the pudding according to package directions.

3. Spoon the pudding over the angel food cake.

4. Top with Cool Whip®. Sprinkle with the candy.

5. Chill.

Dirt Dessert

Some people might be turned off by the name of this dessert. But don't worry—the taste will definitely change their minds!

(Serves plenty)

You'll need:

1 large package Oreo® cookies
one 12-ounce container Cool Whip®
8 ounces cream cheese, softened
1 cup powdered sugar
1 stick margarine, softened
2 cups milk
one 3-ounce box French vanilla pudding
1 teaspoon vanilla
Gummy Worms®

1. Place Oreos® in a zippered plastic bag. [STOP] Use a kitchen mallet to crush them. Place half of them in the bottom of an 11-inch x 17-inch pan.

2. [STOP] Use a mixer to blend Cool Whip®, cream cheese, powdered sugar, and margarine.

3. In a separate bowl, combine pudding, milk, and vanilla. [STOP] Beat this mixture until it looks and feels like pudding.

4. Combine the pudding and Cool Whip® mixtures. Pour this over the layer of crushed cookies.

5. Sprinkle the rest of the Oreos® on the top. Garnish with Gummy Worms®.

6. Refrigerate until serving time.

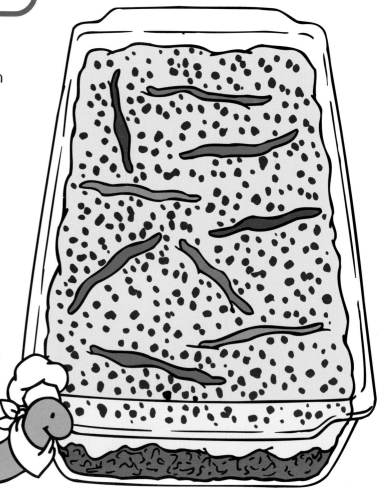

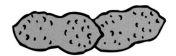

Peanut Butter Balls

You can magically whip up a batch of these tasties in no time.

(Makes 50)

You'll need:
2 cups peanut butter
1 cup rolled oats
1 cup powdered milk
1 cup raisins
1/4 cup honey

1. Mix all the ingredients together in a bowl.

2. Form the mixture into teaspoon-size balls.

3. You are ready to eat!

Chocolate Cream Dream

This is an easy version of Grandma's chocolate cream pie.

(Serves 6)

You'll need:

1/4 cup smooth peanut butter
1 Tablespoon plus 1 teaspoon honey
2-1/4 ounces crisp rice cereal
1 package chocolate pudding mix
2 cups milk
1 small container Cool Whip®

5. Prepare the chocolate pudding with milk, according to the directions on the package. Pour the pudding into the crust.

6. Refrigerate for one hour (do not cover). Spread the Cool Whip® over the top.

1. Combine the peanut butter and honey in a bowl.

2. Stir in the rice cereal. Mix well so the cereal gets evenly coated by the peanut butter and honey.

3. Spray an eight-inch square pan with nonstick cooking spray. With the back of a spoon, press the cereal mixture into the bottom of the pan.

4. Freeze for 30 minutes (do not cover).

Fun Food Fact: Cacao beans, which are used to make chocolate, were once used as money in South America.

Easy Raisin Bars

Mom and Dad will love this snack because it's healthful.
You'll just love the way it tastes!

(Makes 20 bars)

You'll need:
3-1/4 cups graham cracker crumbs
1 cup raisins
2 cups unsweetened crispy rice cereal
one 14-ounce can sweetened
    condensed milk

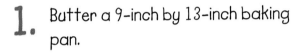

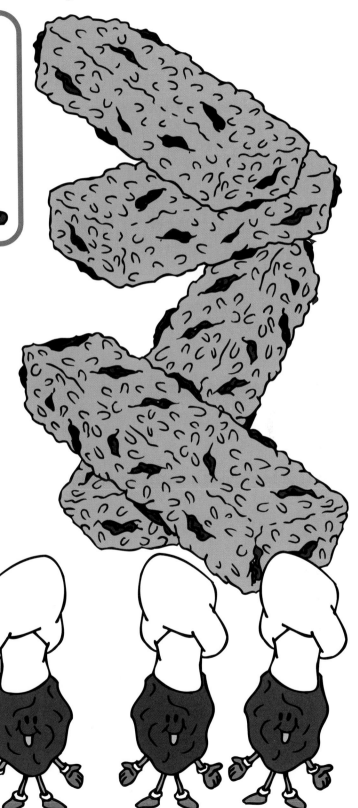

1. Butter a 9-inch by 13-inch baking pan.

2. In a bowl, combine the graham cracker crumbs, raisins, and cereal. Stir well.

3. Add the milk and stir. (Use your hands if it's easier.)

4. Spread the mixture into the pan. Use your hands or the back of a spoon to press it down.

5. Let stand 15 minutes before cutting. Cut into 20 bars.

Holiday Yummies

What's a holiday without food? Valentine candy hearts, Easter eggs, Fourth of July picnics, Halloween trick-or-treating, Thanksgiving turkey, Hanukkah chocolate coins?

Your family probably has special meals and cakes and cookies that you enjoy on certain holidays. Here's a bunch of recipes for sweet snacks that you can make a part of your holiday celebrations. Some can also be used as decorations or gifts. Some are just made for plain good eating! So let's get cookin' and have a Happy New Year! And a Happy St. Patrick's Day! And a Happy (but scary!) Halloween! And a Happy Hanukkah! And a Merry Christmas! And...

Yummy Shamrocks

Top o' the morning to you! This St. Patrick's Day treat is proof that cornflakes aren't just for breakfast anymore.

(How many depends on the size of the shamrocks)

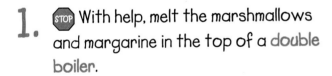

You'll need:

35 marshmallows
1 stick margarine
1 teaspoon vanilla
3 cups cornflakes
1 teaspoon green food coloring
green sprinkles

1. **STOP** With help, melt the marshmallows and margarine in the top of a double boiler.

2. Add the vanilla, coloring, and cornflakes.

3. Let the mixture cool slightly. Form shamrocks as shown on small sheets of waxed paper.

4. Decorate with green candy sprinkles.

 # Jell-O® Salad Egg on Coconut

This Easter snack is as much fun to make as it is to eat. Make the eggs the day before you plan to prepare this salad. So what are you waiting for? Hop to it!

(Makes 7-8 eggs)

You'll need:
9 eggs (8 to blow out the insides and save the unbroken shells)
one 3-ounce package Jell-O®
1 cup boiling water
1/2 cup milk
shredded coconut
green food coloring

1. Make a small pinhole in the top of one egg; then make a slightly larger hole in the bottom. Blow into the small hole until the eggshell is completely empty (if you have a hard time getting the egg out, make holes slightly larger). Do the same for seven more eggs (you should have one left over). Gently run hot water through each shell to clean the inside out.

2. Put a small piece of tape over the smaller hole on the top of each egg.

3. **STOP** Ask a grown-up to boil the water. Dissolve the Jell-O® in the boiling water.

4. **STOP** With help, beat the last egg and the milk together with an electric mixer.

5. Take the Jell-O® off the stove and let it cool slightly. Add the egg-milk mixture.

6. Fill the empty shells with this mixture. Stand them in an egg carton and refrigerate them overnight.

7. To serve, peel the eggshells away.

8. Place the coconut in a small container with a lid. Add food coloring to the coconut and shake the container until the coconut has changed color.

9. Sprinkle the coconut onto a serving plate. Lay the eggs on top.

Fun Food Fact: This Jell-O® salad may be worthy of ancient Rome; the Romans would often decorate their food with pearls and other jewels, because the look of the food was very important. At one banquet, an "egg" made of pastry opened to reveal a tiny cooked bird.

84

Pumpkin-Shaped Snacks

These crunchy munchies give new meaning to the words "Great Pumpkin."

(Makes 10)

You'll need:

3 cups of miniature marshmallows
1/4 cup margarine*
red and yellow food coloring
5 cups Apple Cinnamon Cheerios®
10 green gumdrops

1. Put the marshmallows and margarine in a large saucepan. (STOP) Warm the mixture on the stovetop over low heat until the marshmallows melt.

2. Stir in a few drops of red and yellow food coloring to make the mixture orange.

3. Fold in the Cheerios®.

4. When the mixture has cooled enough, lightly coat your hands with vegetable oil cooking spray.

5. Measure out 1/2 cup of the mixture and shape it into a pumpkin form. Press a green gumdrop into the pumpkin for a stem. Repeat to make ten pumpkins.

6. Set the pumpkins on waxed paper until they become firm.

*1 stick margarine = 1/2 cup margarine = 8 Tablespoons margarine

Chef's Secret: When baking, use only butter or margarine sticks. Butter that comes in tubs has a lot of air and water in it, so it won't measure out correctly and your recipe will come out dry.

No-Bake Spider Cookies

These Halloween cookies will disappear so fast
you'll think they have legs (and they do!).

(Makes 2 to 3 dozen cookies)

You'll need:

2 cups sugar
1/4 cup margarine*
1/2 cup milk
3 cups rolled oats
4 Tablespoons cocoa
3/4 cup peanut butter
1 teaspoon vanilla
1 package string licorice
1 package M&M's®

1. Mix the sugar, margarine, and milk in a saucepan.

2. **STOP** With help, heat the mixture on the stovetop until it boils.

3. Remove the pan from the heat. Stir in the rolled oats, cocoa, peanut butter, and vanilla.

4. After it has cooled, form the mixture into rounded, spider-shaped mounds on waxed paper.

5. Tear each piece of licorice into eight equal pieces. Push the licorice pieces into the "spider bodies" to look like legs.

6. Use two M&M's® as the eyes for each spider.

7. Refrigerate the cookies until firm.

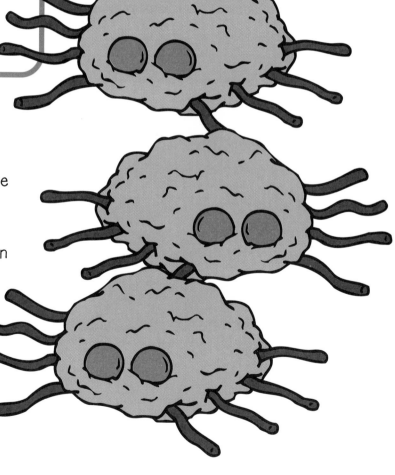

*1 stick margarine = 1/2 cup margarine = 8 Tablespoons margarine

Monster Mash

At your next Halloween bash,
Give the menu some dash,
And serve all your friends
This cool Monster Mash!

(Serves 1)

You'll need:

1 scoop Boo Goo (vanilla ice cream)
1 Tablespoon Swamp Mud
(chocolate syrup)
1 Tablespoon Spider Fangs
(mini chocolate chips)
10 Mummy Toes (miniature marshmallows)
a spoonful of Ghost Guts
(whipped topping)
a few drops of Witches' Brew
(green food coloring)

1. Place the Boo Goo, Swamp Mud, Spider Fangs, and Mummy Toes in a paper cup.

2. Mash them together with a spoon.

3. To make Snake Slime: In another cup, mix a drop or two of the Witches' Brew with a spoonful of the Ghost Guts.

4. Top the Monster Mash with the Snake Slime.

Turkey Treats

These little turkeys are not only good to eat,
they are a fun way to decorate Mom's Thanksgiving table.

(Makes 1)

You'll need:

1 Oreo® cookie
1 piece candy corn
1 Brach's® chocolate creme drop
1 Fudge Stripe® cookie
chocolate frosting

1. Lay the Oreo® on the table. Put a drop of frosting on the back outer edge of the cookie as shown.

2. To make tail feathers, attach the Fudge Stripe® cookie to the Oreo® (with the drop of frosting).

3. Put a drop of frosting on the Oreo®, in front of the Fudge Stripe® cookie.

4. To make the body, put the Brach's® chocolate creme drop on top of that dot of frosting.

5. Put a small bit of frosting on top of the chocolate creme drop.

6. To make the turkey's beak, put one piece of candy corn on top of the chocolate creme drop, pointing away from Fudge Stripe® cookie.

Frosting

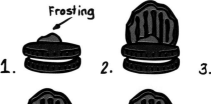

1.   2.   3.

4.   5.   6.

Fun Food Fact: The first Thanksgiving meal was served at breakfast time.

Personal Pumpkin Pie

Save some time this Thanksgiving—whip up a batch of these
mini pies instead of baking one big one.

(Makes 1)

You'll need:
1/4 cup vanilla pudding
1 teaspoon canned pumpkin
dash of pumpkin pie spice
1 single-serving-size
   graham cracker crust
1 small pumpkin-shaped piece of candy

1. Prepare vanilla pudding according to the directions on the package.

2. In a small bowl, mix the pudding, canned pumpkin, and the pumpkin pie spice. Stir well.

3. Spoon the mixture into the prepared crust.

4. Chill.

5. Decorate with the pumpkin candy.

Fun Food Fact: In 1992, a group of people in Nut Tree, California, carved a jack-o'-lantern from an 827-pound pumpkin! Then, in 1994, a man in Ontario, Canada, grew a pumpkin that weighed in at 990 pounds!

Candy Christmas Trees

These snacks make fun table decorations for holiday parties.

(Each cone makes 1 tree)

You'll need:
vanilla frosting
green food coloring
sugar cones
gumdrops, peppermints, M&M's®,
    other small candies

1. Add food coloring to the frosting until it is the shade of green you like.

2. Using a plastic knife, cover a sugar cone with the icing.

3. Put the cone over two or three of your fingers.

4. Press candy pieces into the icing to decorate your tree.

5. Let your tree stand for awhile until the icing is firm.

Careful Cooking: Never leave knives and other kitchen tools lying around where a younger brother or sister might grab them.

Reindeer Refreshments

This year, after leaving out the cookies for Santa,
why not make a little snack for Rudolph and the gang?

(Serves 1)

You'll need:

1/2 cup granola

5 chocolate chips

10 shelled peanuts

15 M&M's®

20 raisins

1. Mix all the ingredients together.

2. Pour the reindeer food into a bowl.

3. Leave the bowl near a door on December 24.

4. Check the bowl in the morning!

5. Enjoy the leftovers!

Fun Food Fact: M&M's® were created for the army by Forrest Mars and Bruce Murries in 1940.

Ready-to-Eat Christmas Wreaths

Wrap these wreaths in Saran Wrap® and use them as package toppers and Christmas tree ornaments!

(How many depends on the size of the wreaths)

You'll need:

35 marshmallows
1 stick margarine
1 teaspoon vanilla extract
1 teaspoon green food coloring
3 cups cornflakes
cinnamon red hots

1. **STOP** With help, melt the marshmallows and margarine in a double boiler.

2. Add vanilla, food coloring, and cornflakes.

3. Form the mixture into wreath shapes on waxed paper.

4. Press cinnamon candies into the wreaths for berries.

5. Let the wreaths stand until firm.

Optional: For a festive touch, tie big bows around your wreaths.

Fun Food Fact: One of America's favorite breakfast foods was discovered by accident. W. K. Kellogg was experimenting with grain—cooking it, running it through rollers, and grinding up the rolled dough—but it kept coming out too mushy. One day, he left the grain on the stove too long and it dried up. He rolled it out anyway and the grain turned into yummy flakes—cornflakes.

Meals Mom & Dad Will Love

Every day, at dinnertime, millions of different kinds of foods are served all over the world. Don't worry that the meals you make are not fancy enough or special enough. Mom and Dad will think these recipes are delicious because you make them! And that's a really big deal because, let's face it, they won't let you cook what they don't want to eat. The meals in this section are quick and easy to save you time. They are simple enough for you to do most of the cooking yourself. So tie on an apron, grab your spatula, and let's get started!

Meatloaf

After Mom tastes your meatloaf, she'll never make her plain old recipe again!

(Serves 6–8)

You'll need:
1/2 cup canned tomato sauce
1-1/2 cups bread crumbs
1 egg, beaten
2 pounds ground beef
2 teaspoons salt
dash of pepper
1 cup hot water
1 cup instant mashed potato flakes
3/4 cup shredded cheddar cheese*

1. **STOP** Ask a grown-up to preheat the oven to 350°.

2. In a bowl, combine the tomato sauce, bread crumbs, and egg. Stir well.

3. Add the ground beef, salt, and pepper. Mix well (you can use your hands for best results!).

4. Transfer the meat mixture into a loaf pan. Smooth the top with your hand or the back of a spoon.

5. **STOP** Cook the meatloaf for one hour.

6. In a bowl, combine hot water and instant potatoes. Stir and mix well.

7. Spread the potatoes on top of the meatloaf when it is done. **STOP** Cook the meatloaf for another 15 minutes.

8. Sprinkle with the cheese and cook until the cheese has melted.

*4 ounces cheddar or mozzarella = 1 cup

Tip: For a healthy change of pace, substitute ground turkey for the ground beef.

Saucy Skillet Dinner

You will love the easy cleanup for this recipe. Everything is cooked in one skillet, so there's almost no mess!

(Serves 4)

You'll need:
1 pound ground beef
1 envelope beef-flavored onion soup mix
1-1/4 cups water
one 8-ounce can tomato sauce
one 7-ounce can corn
3/4 cup uncooked elbow macaroni
1/2 cup shredded cheddar cheese*

1. STOP Ask a grown-up to brown the beef in a large skillet; then drain.

2. Stir in the soup mix, water, tomato sauce, corn, and macaroni.

3. STOP With help, bring the mixture to a boil; then cover. Let it simmer for about 18 minutes or until the macaroni is tender. Stir occasionally.

4. Top with the cheese.

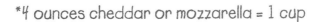

*4 ounces cheddar or mozzarella = 1 cup

Sloppy Joes

A sophisticated television character* once called these "Untidy Josephs," but no matter what name you use, we're sure you'll call them delicious!

(Makes 6)

You'll need:
1 pound ground beef
1 onion, chopped
1 garlic clove, minced
1 large green pepper, chopped
one 30-ounce jar of tomato sauce
6 hamburger rolls

1. **STOP** Ask an adult to help you brown the beef in a **skillet**. With help, drain the grease off the meat.

2. Add the onion, garlic, peppers, and tomato sauce.

3. Cover. **STOP** **Simmer** on medium heat for 45 minutes.

4. **STOP** Toast the hamburger rolls.

5. Serve the meat mixture on the hamburger rolls.

*Trivia: This would be the butler, Mr. French, on "Family Affair."

Fun Food Fact: Chopped meat patties were first cooked in Hamburg, Germany, where they were called "Deutsche" or "beefsteak." When they came to America, they were known as "Hamburg steaks" and then "Hamburgers."

Easy Barbecue

This spicy dinner is perfect for a backyard picnic or Fourth of July celebration.

(Serves 6-8)

You'll need:
2 pounds ground beef
1/2 mango, chopped
3 Tablespoons vinegar
3 Tablespoons sugar
1 onion, chopped
12 ounces ketchup
2 Tablespoons mustard
hamburger rolls

1. **STOP** Ask a grown-up to brown the meat in a skillet or saucepan.

2. Add the other ingredients.

3. **STOP** Let the mixture simmer for 45 minutes to an hour.

4. Serve on hamburger rolls.

Fun Food Fact: Ketchup came from China. The Chinese made a sauce from fish broth and mushrooms that they called "ke-tsiap." Sailors brought the recipe to England where tomatoes were thrown into the mixture. The English called the sauce "kechup."

Beefy Chili Mac

This dish is a big favorite of dads everywhere. So don't be shy about asking him to be your kitchen assistant.

(Serves 4)

You'll need:
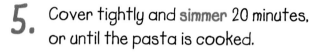

1 pound ground beef
1 Tablespoon vegetable oil
1 onion, chopped
2 cans (14-1/2 ounces each) chili-seasoned
    diced tomatoes, undrained
1-1/2 cups uncooked rotini (spiral) pasta
1/2 cup water
1/2 cup shredded cheddar cheese*

5. Cover tightly and **simmer** 20 minutes, or until the pasta is cooked.

6. Sprinkle with cheese and serve.

1. **STOP** Ask a grown-up to help you heat the oil in a saucepan over medium-high heat until it's hot.

2. Add the ground beef and the onion. **STOP** Cook, while stirring, for three minutes.

3. Add the tomatoes, pasta, and water to the beef and stir well.

4. **STOP** Bring the mixture to a boil. Reduce heat to low.

*4 ounces cheddar or mozzarella = 1 cup

Careful Cooking: Steam can burn, so stand back and use a pot holder when you are taking the lids off baking dishes and pots.

Burger Surprise

These stuffed, "barbecue-y" burgers are an unexpected treat!

(Serves 4)

You'll need:
1-1/2 pounds ground beef
1 teaspoon salt
1/4 teaspoon black pepper
2 Tablespoons barbecue sauce
4 slices cheddar cheese
4 hamburger buns

1. In a bowl, mix the beef, salt, and pepper.

2. Divide the mixture into four equal parts. Now take each of those parts and divide them in half (you will have eight portions of beef).

3. On a piece of waxed paper, pat down each portion of beef into a four-inch pattie.

4. Spread the barbecue sauce on four of the burger patties.

5. Place a slice of cheddar cheese on top of each of the patties with the sauce.

6. Put one plain pattie on top of each cheese pattie. Pinch the edges of each pattie to seal the cheese and sauce inside.

7. STOP Cook immediately. Ask a grown-up to heat the broiler pan and broil the burgers six inches from the heat. Cook each for about six to eight minutes on each side. Serve on the hamburger buns.

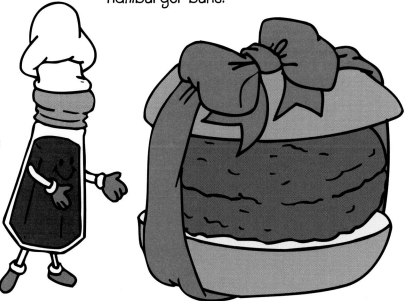

Tip: For a special treat, ask Dad to cook the burgers on the barbecue grill outside. Dads love to grill!

Fun Food Fact: Did you know that McDonald's® is opening restaurants in countries like India where it is illegal for them to sell hamburgers? In India, the cow is a sacred animal and cannot be eaten.

Tater Tot Casserole

Everyone's favorite side dish becomes the main meal in this tasty concoction.

(Serves 4-6)

You'll need:
1 to 1-1/2 pounds ground beef
1 can cream of celery soup
1 onion, chopped
1 package frozen Ore Ida® Tater Tots potatoes
salt and pepper

1. Press the ground beef into the bottom of a 9-inch square glass dish.

2. Sprinkle salt, pepper, and the chopped onions on the meat.

3. Pour the soup over the meat.

4. Add a layer of Tater Tots.

5. **STOP** Cover and bake at 350° for 40 minutes.

6. Uncover the casserole and bake until the potatoes are crispy.

Fun Food Fact: Up until the Middle Ages, one communal dish was shared by everyone at the table. During the Middle Ages, diners started using bowls made for two people at a time. Few people used individual plates before the 1700s.

Turkey Sloppy Joes

Here's a nifty twist on a classic school cafeteria meal.

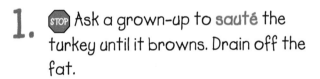

(Serves 4)

You'll need:
1 pound ground turkey
two 8-ounce cans tomato sauce
1 package sloppy joe seasoning mix
toasted hamburger buns

1. **STOP** Ask a grown-up to **sauté** the turkey until it browns. Drain off the fat.

2. Add the tomato sauce and seasoning mix.

3. With help, let the mixture **simmer** for 20 minutes.

4. Spoon on toasted hamburger buns and serve.

Careful Cooking: Never put cooked chicken or turkey back in the same dish you used before they were cooked. Raw poultry can spread salmonella bacteria, which can make you sick.

Taco-Turkey Pie

With a little help, this cheesy Mexican-flavored dish
will be sizzling in the oven in no time!

(Serves 4-6)

You'll need:

8 refrigerated biscuits
1 pound ground turkey
1 package taco seasoning mix
3/4 cup water
3/4 cup salsa
6 ounces cheese*

1. Spray a 9-inch pie plate with cooking spray.

2. Roll the biscuits between two pieces of waxed paper.

3. Mold the resulting dough into the pie plate.

4. (STOP) Ask an adult to brown the meat.

5. Add the taco seasoning mix, water, and salsa to the meat. (STOP) With help, cook the meat until the mixture is heated through.

6. Place a layer of the meat mixture in the pie plate. Follow with a layer of cheese.

7. Repeat the layering, ending with a layer of cheese.

8. (STOP) With Mom's help, bake the pie at 400° for ten minutes.

*4 ounces cheddar or mozzarella = 1 cup

Fun Food Fact: During the 1300s, the fork was a symbol of wealth and only used once in awhile by members of royalty (who may have owned one or two). It wasn't until the 1700s, in France, that most people began eating with forks.

Turkey Burgers

Stand back and watch as these burgers are gobbled up!

(Makes 4)

You'll need:
1 pound ground turkey
2 Tablespoons minced onion
3/4 teaspoon soy sauce
1-1/4 teaspoons Dijon mustard
dash of black pepper
4 hamburger buns

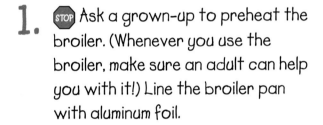

1. STOP Ask a grown-up to preheat the broiler. (Whenever you use the broiler, make sure an adult can help you with it!) Line the broiler pan with aluminum foil.

2. Combine the turkey, onion, soy sauce, mustard, and pepper. Use your hands to mix it well.

3. Make four turkey burger patties out of the mix.

4. STOP Ask a grown-up helper to place the patties on the broiler pan. Tell your helper to broil your burgers, two inches from the heat, until they are cooked through (this should take about five minutes on each side).

5. Serve the burgers on the hamburger buns with lettuce and tomato. Put a little salsa on top for extra zing!

Fun Food Fact: If you think turkey burgers are strange, how about this? The first "hamburgers" were eaten by the Tartars, a Mongol people, in 13 A.D. The burgers were made of raw, shredded goat, camel, or horse meat!

Baked Reuben

This clever recipe turns a favorite sandwich into a hot, welcoming casserole for your whole family.

(Serves 4)

You'll need:

2 Tablespoons mayonnaise
1 Tablespoon chili sauce
1 Tablespoon vinegar
2 cups sauerkraut (thoroughly drained)
2 slices rye bread, torn into small pieces
2 large tomatoes, sliced
6 ounces ham or turkey ham, sliced
3 ounces grated Swiss cheese
1 ounce grated Swiss cheese

1. To make the dressing, mix mayonnaise, chili sauce, and vinegar in a bowl.

2. Coat a square baking pan with nonstick cooking spray.

3. Place the sauerkraut in the pan. On top of the sauerkraut, layer the tomatoes, ham, and three ounces of cheese (in that order).

4. **STOP** Pour the dressing on top. With help, bake the casserole at 350° for 15 minutes.

5. Remove from the oven; sprinkle with bread pieces and the remaining ounce of cheese.

6. **STOP** Bake for 15 more minutes.

Fun Food Fact: Sauerkraut is a tangy cabbage dish. Cabbage is soaked in a brine made of its own juice and salt. Many countries have similar cabbage recipes, including Korea, where "kimchi" is the national dish.

Sunny Chicken Salad

This chicken salad will surprise you with sweet and juicy bursts of flavor.

(Serves 4)

You'll need:

9 ounces cooked chicken, cubed
12 grapes, cut in half
1 banana, sliced
1 orange, peeled and sectioned
1 ounce walnuts
1/4 cup mayonnaise
2 cups shredded lettuce

1. Combine all ingredients except lettuce. Toss gently to mix well.

2. To serve, arrange lettuce on a plate. Spoon the chicken salad on top.

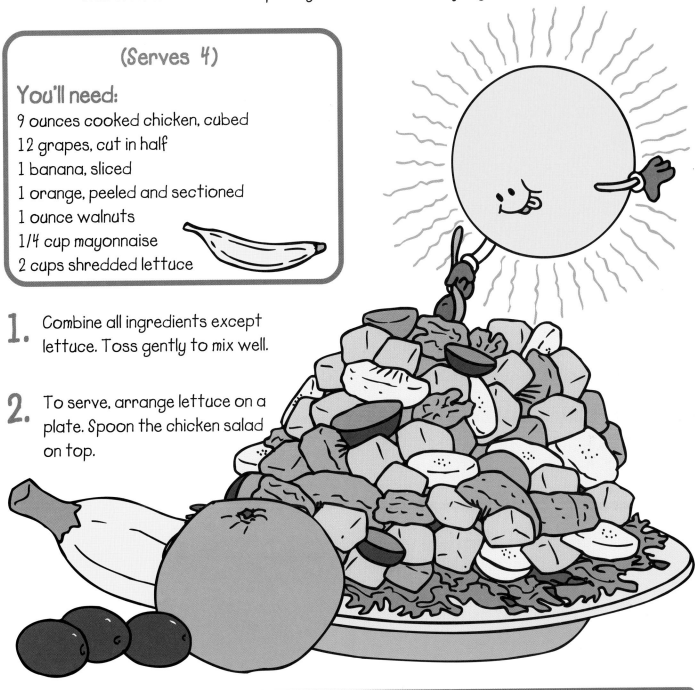

Fun Food Fact: New Zealand is an island nation. The traditional Christmas meal is a picnic on one of its beaches because in December New Zealand is having summer.

Quick Chicken Cordon Bleu

Your family will be impressed when you
whip up this elegant but easy dinner.

(Serves 1)

You'll need:
1 deboned chicken breast
1 ounce shredded mozzarella cheese*
garlic powder
fresh parsley
2 Tablespoons diced ham (optional)
salt and pepper
seasoned bread crumbs

1. (STOP) With help, use a meat mallet to pound the chicken breast to about 1/2-inch thickness.

2. Fill the breast with a mixture of mozzarella cheese, garlic powder, parsley, and diced ham.

3. Add salt and pepper to taste.

4. Roll up the breast and insert a toothpick to secure.

5. Pour some bread crumbs in a shallow dish. Dip the rolled breast in the crumbs.

6. (STOP) Bake the chicken at 350° for 25 minutes.

*4 ounces cheddar or mozzarella = 1 cup

Careful Cooking: When you make chicken or turkey, be sure you wash your hands in hot, soapy water. Also wash the cutting board, the knife, and any other kitchen tools or countertops that came in contact with the poultry. Raw poultry carries salmonella bacteria that can make you sick.

Chicken à la Fast

You'll hear clucks of praise when you set your version
of Chicken à la King on the table.

(Serves 4)

You'll need:
two 14-1/2-ounce cans chicken broth
1/2 cup milk
1/4 to 1/2 cup flour
1 chicken bouillon cube
1 teaspoon sage
dash of pepper
2 cups cut-up chicken, cooked
1-1/2 cups frozen mixed vegetables,
   cooked and drained
8 slices of bread, toasted

1. (STOP) Ask a grown-up to heat the chicken broth in a **skillet**.

2. In a small bowl, mix the milk and flour to make a paste.

3. Add the paste to the broth.

4. Crush the bouillon cube into the skillet.

5. Stir in the sage and pepper.

6. (STOP) Bring to a boil; then let the mixture **simmer** to thicken into a sauce.

7. Add the chicken and vegetables.

8. (STOP) Simmer for 10 to 15 minutes.

9. Spoon the mixture over the toasted bread slices to serve.

Fun Food Fact: "Colonel" Harland Sanders was a ferryboat pilot, train conductor, farmer, soldier, and salesman before opening a gas station on a Kentucky highway. When people dropped by at dinnertime, he would feed them, too. His fried chicken was very popular. He made it with a secret recipe of 11 spices. The Colonel's chicken was so popular, in fact, that he opened his own restaurant—*Kentucky Fried Chicken*®.

107

 # Chicken and Rice Casserole

Throw together this easy dinner in the blink of an eye!

(Serves 4)

You'll need:
2 cups cooked rice (or 1 cup uncooked Minute® Brand rice)
1 large can chunky chicken
1 can cream of mushroom soup
1/4 cup margarine, melted*
1/2 cup grated cheese**

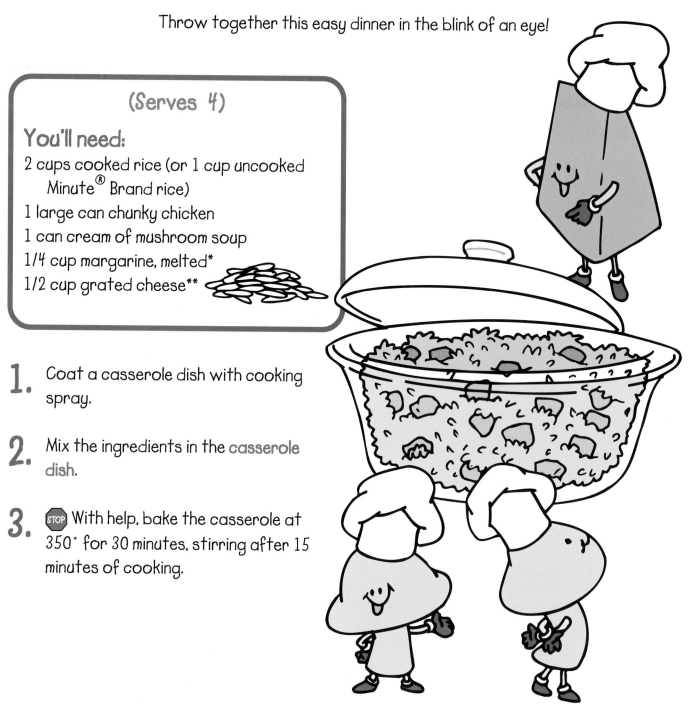

1. Coat a casserole dish with cooking spray.

2. Mix the ingredients in the casserole dish.

3. (STOP) With help, bake the casserole at 350° for 30 minutes, stirring after 15 minutes of cooking.

*1 stick margarine = 1/2 cup margarine = 8 Tablespoons margarine
**3-ounce block of Parmesan cheese = 1/2 cup grated cheese

Fun Food Fact: Every year in June, the Japanese celebrate the Day of the Rice God. This rice-transplanting festival is hundreds of years old and was revived in the 1930s. Along with dancing, parades, and music, it includes prayers to the Shinto rice god, Wbai-sama.

Microwave Italian Chicken

Mamma mia! Here's a quick Italian feast!

(Serves about 6)

You'll need:
6 to 10 chicken breasts or thighs, skinned
Italian-seasoned bread crumbs
melted butter
Parmesan cheese

1. Place the bread crumbs in a shallow bowl.

2. Use your hands to quickly dip the chicken pieces in butter. (After you've dipped the chicken, hold the pieces over the bowl of butter for a few seconds to drain away the extra.)

3. Roll the chicken pieces in the bread crumbs.

4. Place the chicken in a microwaveable baking dish and sprinkle with the cheese.

5. **STOP** Microwave for 10 to 20 minutes on high (depending on the number of chicken pieces). Rotate the dish every five minutes of cooking time.

Careful Cooking: When you cook chicken or turkey, it is done when the juices that run out of the meat are clear. Also, when you cut into the meat or pull it away from the bones, it should be white, not pink or red.

Homemade Tortillas

This Mexican food can be used to create other Mexican dishes, but you can also use it to serve chicken salad, make a pizza, or eat as part of your breakfast. How many ways can you think of to use a tortilla?

(Makes 12 small tortillas)

You'll need:
1 cup corn flour
1 teaspoon salt
3/4 to 1 cup warm water

1. Place all the ingredients in a bowl and mix together.

2. Divide dough into 12 balls.

3. Press each ball between two sheets of waxed paper to flatten.

4. Peel away waxed paper. **STOP** Ask a grown-up helper to place the tortilla on an ungreased, heated griddle.

5. **STOP** Flip tortilla when edges begin to brown.

6. Remove from heat when edges are brown.

7. Do the same for the remaining balls of dough.

Fun Food Fact: A 3,960-pound burrito was made in 1994 in Montebello, California. It was made with eggs, refried beans, cheese, tomatoes, lettuce, and salsa. The tortilla that held it all together was over 3,055 feet long!

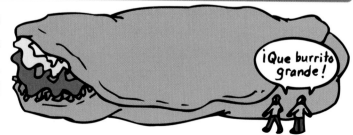

¡Que burrito grande!

Quesadillas

This Mexican dish can be served as a meal, a side dish, an appetizer, or a snack.

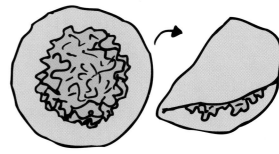

(Makes 12)

You'll need:
12 tortillas
12 ounces cheddar cheese, shredded*

1. **STOP** Ask an adult to heat a tortilla on the griddle for about five seconds.

2. Flip the tortilla.

3. Sprinkle one ounce of cheese on the tortilla.

4. Carefully fold the tortilla in half.

5. **STOP** With help, heat the quesadilla until the cheese melts.

6. Repeat this process with the remaining tortillas.

*4 ounces cheddar or mozzarella = 1 cup

Tacos

Cook up a batch of these to celebrate the big Mexican holiday called Cinco de Mayo (that's May 5th!), or to celebrate any day when you're in a festive mood.

(Makes 6 tacos)

You'll need:

1 pound ground beef
1 cup taco sauce or tomato sauce
6 taco shells
shredded cheddar cheese
shredded lettuce
diced tomatoes
diced onion
salsa
salt and pepper

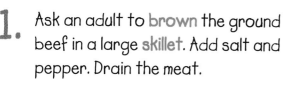

1. Ask an adult to brown the ground beef in a large skillet. Add salt and pepper. Drain the meat.

2. Add the taco sauce.

3. STOP With help, heat the skillet on *medium*, until the mixture is warmed through.

4. STOP Warm the taco shells in the oven for five minutes at 250°. (Shells will soften a bit.)

5. Spoon the beef mixture into the shells.

6. Top the tacos with whatever you like: cheese, lettuce, tomatoes, onions, salsa. You can also serve them with sour cream and guacamole.

Tip: This is another recipe where ground turkey can replace the ground beef for a tasty change of pace.

Fun Food Fact: Guacamole is a dip made with mashed avocados, and is sometimes served on tortilla chips, tacos, enchiladas, and quesadillas.

Taco Salad

This clever twist on a Mexican favorite should convince
Mom and Dad to eat their vegetables.

(Serves 4)

You'll need:

1 pound ground beef
1 Tablespoon vegetable oil
1/2 cup chopped yellow onion
2 garlic cloves, minced
1/4 teaspoon ground cumin (optional)
2 heads of any kind of lettuce
1 red onion, thinly sliced
8 cherry tomatoes, each cut in 4 pieces
1 cup crumbled tortilla chips
1 cup shredded cheddar cheese*
1/2 cup chunky salsa

1. (STOP) With help, cook the ground beef in a large nonstick **skillet** over medium-high heat. Stir occasionally, until the meat is no longer pink. It will take about five minutes.

2. (STOP) Pour the meat into a **colander** to drain off the fat.

3. (STOP) Wipe the fat out of the skillet with a paper towel.

4. (STOP) With help, heat the vegetable oil in the skillet over medium-high heat.

5. Add the yellow onion, garlic, and cumin. Cook until the onion gets soft, about five minutes.

6. Stir in the beef. Cook for five more minutes.

7. Rinse the lettuce leaves and pat them dry with a paper towel. Tear the leaves into bite-size pieces. Place some of the lettuce on each serving plate.

8. Top each plate of lettuce with some of the beef. Sprinkle each plate with the rings of red onion, the tomatoes, the chips, and the cheddar cheese. Put a little salsa on top of each salad.

*4 ounces cheddar or mozzarella = 1 cup

South-of-the-Border Casserole

This spicy dish combines all the great tastes of Mexican food in one bite.

(Serves 3-4)

You'll need:
1 pound lean ground beef
2 teaspoons dried minced onion
2 teaspoons dried minced garlic
1 teaspoon chili powder
1 cup chunky-style salsa
2/3 cup crushed corn chips
shredded cheddar cheese

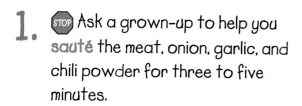

1. **STOP** Ask a grown-up to help you **sauté** the meat, onion, garlic, and chili powder for three to five minutes.

2. Remove the meat mixture from the heat. Stir in the salsa.

3. Spread the mixture in a **casserole dish.**

4. Top with the crushed corn chips.

5. **STOP** With help, bake the casserole for ten minutes in a 350° oven.

6. Sprinkle the cheddar cheese over the top and bake until the cheese melts (about five minutes).

Fun Food Fact: The ancient Egyptians thought onions kept evil spirits away. If they took an oath during a ceremony, they placed one hand on an onion.

Excellent Enchiladas

This is a fun and delicious meal to make when friends stay for dinner.

(Makes 8 enchiladas)

You'll need:

8 tortillas

1 pound cooked and shredded chicken, or three to four 5-ounce cans of chicken

8 ounces shredded cheddar cheese*

1 cup sour cream

salsa (optional)

oil

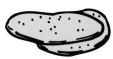

1. Grease the skillet with a teaspoon of oil.

2. [STOP] With help, heat the skillet on medium-high heat.

3. Put a small amount of chicken in each tortilla; top each with a spoonful of sour cream.

4. Fold up both sides of the tortilla.

5. [STOP] Place the enchilada in the skillet, seam side down.

6. Repeat steps 3 through 5 for the rest of the tortillas.

7. Sprinkle the enchiladas with cheese.

8. [STOP] With help, cook the enchiladas for 15 to 20 minutes.

9. Serve each individual enchilada with a dollop of sour cream and salsa (if desired).

*4 ounces cheddar or mozzarella = 1 cup

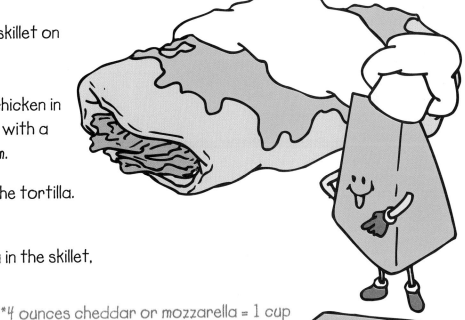

Fun Food Fact: Have you seen the "Cheesemobile"? It was created in 1988 to drive a really big piece of cheese around the United States. The "slice" of cheddar weighed 40,060 pounds and was made in Little Chute, Wisconsin!

Sausage and Rice Casserole

This filling dinner is a snap to make! Just mix everything together and let a grown-up pop it in the oven.

(Serves 4-6)

You'll need:

1 pound hot sausage
1 cup long-grain rice
1 can cream of mushroom soup
1 can consommé
1/2 soup can of water
1 package onion soup mix

optional ingredients:
    1 small can mushrooms
    1/4 cup chopped onion
    1/4 cup chopped green pepper
    1 Tablespoon chopped pimientos

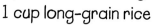

1. **STOP** Ask a grown-up to brown the sausage. Drain off the fat.

2. Add the remaining ingredients and mix thoroughly.

3. Pour the mixture into a two-quart baking dish.

4. **STOP** With help, bake the casserole at 350° for one hour.

Fun Food Fact: In Sheboygan, Wisconsin, people hold a festival that celebrates bratwurst, a kind of sausage. It began in 1953, and the main event is a bratwurst-eating contest.

SHEBOYGAN
ANNUAL BRATWURST FESTIVAL

January Soup

This warm and comforting soup is perfect for cold, snowy nights.
Serve it with some warm biscuits or rolls.

(Makes 7-1/2 cups)

You'll need:

1 can (10-1/2 ounces) condensed,
    old-fashioned vegetable soup
1 can (10-1/2 ounces) condensed
    beef broth
2 soup cans of water
1/2 pound frankfurters, sliced
1/2 cup uncooked small shell macaroni
1/2 cup chopped onion
1 medium green pepper, diced
1/4 cup peanuts
2 Tablespoons chopped parsley
1/4 teaspoon crushed thyme leaves
2 medium tomatoes, diced
generous dash of pepper

1. In a saucepan, combine all ingredients except tomatoes.

2. **STOP** With help, bring the soup to a boil; then reduce the heat.

3. Simmer five minutes or until done. Stir occasionally.

4. Add tomatoes.

5. Let the soup simmer until it is heated through.

Veggie Soup

This delicious soup is so good, you'll forget you're eating your vegetables!

(Serves 6-8)

You'll need:

2 Tablespoons olive oil

3 cups chopped vegetables
(like carrots, celery, tomatoes,
squash, green beans, peas)

6 cups water

6 bouillon cubes

salt and pepper to taste

dash of oregano

1 cup uncooked rice

1 cup drained beans (chickpea,
kidney, or white—your choice)

1. (STOP) Ask a grown-up to heat the olive oil in a large pot.

2. (STOP) Add the vegetables. With help, **sauté** them for about 15 minutes.

3. Add water, bouillon cubes, oregano, and rice.

4. (STOP) Ask your helper to increase the heat and let the soup start boiling. Boil for five minutes.

5. Turn down the heat to let the soup **simmer**. Add the drained beans.

6. Let the soup simmer for 30 minutes.

7. Add salt and pepper until the soup tastes right to you.

Fun Food Fact: In 1990, three men made a wooden bowl that was over 6-1/2 feet tall and 5 feet 9 inches wide. How much veggie soup do you think you'd need to fill it?

Noodle Soup

Let this tasty soup chase away your taste bud blahs!

(Makes about 4 cups)

You'll need:
1 cup shredded carrot
1/2 cup chopped onion
1/2 cup sliced celery
4 teaspoons margarine*
2 cups canned chicken broth
   (ready-to-serve, not condensed)
3 ounces uncooked medium or
   thin egg noodles
1 cup water

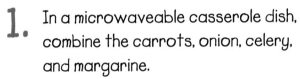

5. Stir in the noodles. Cover and microwave on medium for three minutes (stir once each minute).

6. Let stand for two minutes, until noodles are softened.

1. In a microwaveable casserole dish, combine the carrots, onion, celery, and margarine.

2. Cover and microwave on high for one minute.

3. Add the chicken broth and one cup water. Stir to combine.

4. Cover and microwave on high for five minutes.

*1 stick margarine = 1/2 cup margarine = 8 Tablespoons margarine

Fun Food Fact: In China, Bird's Nest Soup is considered a delicacy and, yes, it is made from real birds' nests, which you can buy in the store.

The whole family can join in making their own personal Saturday night pizzas. Be creative and add any toppings you like.

(Makes 1)

You'll need:

1/4 teaspoon active dry yeast
3 Tablespoons plus 1 teaspoon
    all-purpose flour
1/2 teaspoon olive oil
1/8 teaspoon granulated sugar
1/8 cup jarred tomato sauce
1-1/2 ounces cooked ground beef
3/4 ounce shredded mozzarella cheese*
1-1/2 Tablespoons warm water

1. **STOP** Ask an adult to preheat the oven to 425°.

2. Spray a seven-inch pie plate with nonstick cooking spray.

3. In a bowl, dissolve yeast in the warm water.

4. Add flour, oil, and sugar. Stir until the mixture becomes soft and doughy.

5. Cover the bowl with a towel. Let it sit for five minutes.

6. Press the dough into the pie plate.

7. Spread tomato sauce on the dough. Sprinkle on the cheese and ground beef.

8. **STOP** With help, bake your pizza until the cheese is melted and the crust is browned (about 15 minutes).

*4 ounces cheddar or mozzarella = 1 cup

Tip: You can freeze your pizza after step 7 for an after-school snack. Just cover with plastic wrap and freeze. To cook, place the frozen pizza in the oven and bake for 19 to 21 minutes, or until cheese is melted and crust is browned.

Fun Food Fact: At Chicago's O'Hare International Airport, travelers eat 9,600 slices of the city's famous deep-dish pizza each day!

Micro Mac and Cheese

There are lots of ways to make mac and cheese, but none of them are as quick, creamy, and cheesy as this version.

(Serves 4)

You'll need:

1 Tablespoon plus 1 teaspoon butter
   or margarine*

3 cups cooked elbow macaroni

1/2 cup ricotta cheese

1-1/2 ounces shredded cheddar cheese**

1 Tablespoon plus 1 teaspoon
   grated Parmesan cheese***

1/4 teaspoon pepper

1. **STOP** In a casserole dish, melt butter in the microwave oven (on high, for 30 seconds).

2. Stir in the rest of the ingredients. Mix well.

3. Cover. Microwave on high for three minutes (or until it is heated through).

4. Let stand for one minute before serving.

*1 stick margarine = 1/2 cup margarine = 8 Tablespoons margarine
**4 ounces cheddar or mozzarella = 1 cup
***3-ounce block of Parmesan cheese = 1/2 cup grated cheese

Careful Cooking: When you take a covered dish out of the microwave, use oven mitts and do not stand directly over the dish when you take the lid off. The steam that comes out will be VERY hot and could scald you.

No-Cook Spaghetti Sauce

On top of spaghetti, all covered with cheese,
you pour this quick sauce, prepared with such ease!

(Serves 4)

You'll need:

2 pounds ripe tomatoes
8 to 10 fresh basil leaves,
    washed and chopped
1 garlic clove, peeled and minced (optional)
2 Tablespoons olive oil
1/2 teaspoon salt
1/4 teaspoon black pepper
1 pound spaghetti, uncooked

1. Prepare the sauce about three hours before you are going to eat.

2. **STOP** Ask a grown-up to cut the tomatoes in half and squeeze them over the sink so the juice and the seeds run out.

3. **STOP** With help, cut the tomatoes into small pieces.

4. Put the tomatoes in a bowl. Mix in the basil, garlic, olive oil, salt, and pepper.

5. Cover with plastic wrap. Let the sauce stand. Stir gently a few times.

6. **STOP** Just before you are ready to eat, boil a large pot of water (ask for help). Put the spaghetti into the boiling water. Cook the spaghetti until it is tender.

7. **STOP** Ask your helper to drain the spaghetti into a colander. Save 1/2 cup of the cooking water.

8. Stir the hot water into the tomato mixture. Immediately pour the drained spaghetti on top.

9. Let the spaghetti and sauce stand for about one minute; then toss the pasta well.

Fun Food Fact: Tomatoes, which originated in South America, were brought to Europe in 1596, where they were considered to be deadly poison! Later, Thomas Jefferson grew tomatoes in his garden, but he never ate them. The first harvest of tomatoes was not sold until 1812 at a market in New Orleans.

Blast Off With Breakfast!

Breakfast is an important way to start your day. And it's delicious, too! Whether you are running for the school bus or spending a Sunday morning with your family, breakfast can be the most creative and interesting meal of the day. And it doesn't have to be the morning to enjoy it—try pancakes for a late-night snack or French toast for dinner!

Don't limit yourself to just the recipes in this book. Ask Mom to help you experiment with fruit, eggs, bread, jelly, peanut butter, and any other of your favorite breakfast foods. You'll be thinking up your own delicious surprises in no time.

Chocolate Banana Pancakes

Don't serve these pancakes just for breakfast—
they work just as well for dessert or even for dinner!

(Serves 2)

You'll need:
2 packets of hot chocolate mix
2 bananas, mashed
2 eggs
1/3 cup plus 2 teaspoons flour
2 teaspoons double-acting baking powder
2 teaspoons vanilla extract

1. In a medium bowl, mix together all the ingredients and 1/2 cup of water (use a wire whisk if possible).

2. Spray a **skillet** with nonstick cooking spray. (STOP) Ask an adult to heat the skillet over medium-high heat.

3. Spoon the batter into the skillet (there should be enough for six pancakes).

4. Ask your adult helper to reduce the heat to medium.

5. (STOP) Cook the pancakes until bubbles appear in the batter (about two minutes). Then flip the pancakes with a **spatula**. Cook for about two more minutes.

Fun Food Fact: At Olney, in Buckinghamshire, England, the annual pancake race has been held since 1445. Women wear traditional housewife costumes. While running from the marketplace to the church, they toss and flip the pancakes on the griddles they are carrying.

Baked Pancakes

This is the easiest pancake recipe because there's no hot oil.

(Serves 2)

You'll need:
1/3 cup plus 2 teaspoons buttermilk baking mix
1/4 cup plain yogurt
2 Tablespoons plus 2 teaspoons apricot nectar
1-1/2 teaspoons grated orange peel

1. **STOP** Ask a grown-up to preheat the oven to 400°.

2. Combine all the ingredients. Stir until smooth.

3. Spray nonstick baking sheet with nonstick cooking spray.

4. Drop heaping tablespoons of batter onto the baking sheet, about one inch apart.

5. **STOP** Bake for ten minutes, or until pancakes are browned on bottom.

6. **STOP** With some help, turn the pancakes over. Cook until the other sides are browned, about two minutes.

Fun Food Fact: Pancakes are called many things—hoecakes, flapjacks, griddle cakes, hotcakes, and silver dollars.

Awesome Oatmeal

Say good-bye to instant oatmeal! You won't believe how smooth and creamy this old-fashioned recipe can be.

(Serves 4)

You'll need:

2 cups water
1 cup old-fashioned oats
pinch salt
toppings that you like: milk, syrup, sugar, butter, raisins, bananas, jam

1. Pour the water, oats, and salt into a pot.

2. **STOP** Ask a grown-up to bring the pot to a boil.

3. **STOP** With some help, lower the heat and let the oatmeal **simmer** for five minutes (or until it is as thick as you like it).

4. Serve in bowls with the toppings of your choice.

Fun Food Fact: In Ireland, where Halloween celebrations originated, traditional Halloween foods include raisin bread, baked kale and potatoes, and oatmeal porridge.

Strawberry Jam

If you've never made your own jam, don't miss this traditional recipe.

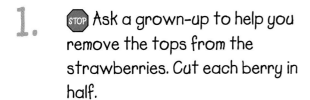

(Makes about 1 cup)

You'll need:
1 pint strawberries
1/2 cup sugar
1 Tablespoon cornstarch
1/2 to 1 teaspoon fresh lemon juice*

1. STOP Ask a grown-up to help you remove the tops from the strawberries. Cut each berry in half.

2. Put the berries in a saucepan. Mash them with a potato masher. Don't let the mix get too "liquidy." (You may also "mash" them in a food processor with a chopping blade—but pulse only a few times until they are in small pieces.)

3. Add sugar to the berries in the saucepan and toss well.

4. Let the mixture stand for 20 minutes.

5. Press a spoon into the berries and remove one tablespoon of the liquid.

6. In a cup, mix the spoonful of berry juice and the cornstarch. Make sure there are no lumps.

7. Add the cornstarch mixture to the berries.

8. STOP With some help, bring the berries to a boil. Continue to boil for 15 minutes, or until the jam is thick. Stir occasionally. (Remember, the jam will thicken up once you put it in the fridge.)

9. When the jam is cool enough to handle, spoon the mixture into a container; then cover and refrigerate.

10. When the mixture is cold, add lemon juice to taste and mix.

*1 lemon = 3 Tablespoons lemon juice

Fun Food Fact: Do you know who Fannie Farmer was? Fannie Farmer was a terrible cook when she was growing up, but she became famous for writing a cookbook. Before Fannie, recipes called for things like "a pinch of salt" and "butter the size of a sugar cube." She was the first cookbook author to use standard measurements.

Breakfast Burrito

This is an unexpected twist on those peanut butter
and jelly sandwiches you love so much!

(Serves 1)

You'll need:

a flour tortilla
1 Tablespoon creamy peanut butter
2 teaspoons strawberry jam
1/2 banana

1. Spread the peanut butter and jam on the tortilla.

2. Roll the tortilla around the banana.

3. Wrap the burrito in a paper towel.

4. **STOP** Microwave on high for 35 seconds.

French Toast

This breakfast is the perfect start to a fun Sunday.

(Serves 4)

You'll need:

3 eggs
1/3 cup milk
dash of cinnamon
dash of vanilla extract
2 Tablespoons margarine*
8 slices bread
powdered sugar

1. **STOP** With help, use an electric mixer to beat the eggs, milk, cinnamon, and vanilla extract together.

2. **STOP** Ask a grown-up to heat a skillet on medium-high heat. Melt the margarine in the skillet.

3. Soak the bread, one slice at a time, in the egg mixture. Make sure you let it soak for only a few seconds on each side.

4. Put two slices of bread in the skillet. **STOP** With some help, cook them on medium heat. Flip them once in awhile so they don't stick or burn.

5. When the slices start to brown, they're done. Now finish up the rest of the bread slices.

6. Sprinkle each slice with a little powdered sugar.

*1 stick margarine = 1/2 cup margarine = 8 Tablespoons margarine

Tip: You can use any type of bread for French toast. Try a thick slice of Italian or French bread. It's terrific!

Veggies and Salads on the Side

Need a little something to go with that chicken or that burger or that meatloaf? Maybe vegetables aren't your favorite things in the world, but there are ways to disguise them and dress them up with other good stuff so you won't even know they're veggies! So don't set the table just yet; add a little something special to your dinner tonight with one of these totally delectable side dishes.

A Different Kind of Macaroni Salad

Impress Mom and Dad with this healthful version of a picnic favorite.

(Serves 4)

You'll need:
2 cups cooked elbow macaroni, chilled
2 hard-boiled eggs, chopped
1/2 cup plain low-fat yogurt
4 Tablespoons chopped red bell pepper
2 Tablespoons chopped scallion
    (green onion)
dash of salt and pepper

1. In a mixing bowl, combine everything. Mix well.

2. Cover and refrigerate at least one hour.

Careful Cooking: Always ask an adult to help you drain things into a colander (like pasta, vegetables, or cooked meat). These foods are steaming hot and sometimes heavy, and the sink can often be just a little out of your reach. The boiling water can cause a really bad burn if you accidentally drop the pot.

Old-Fashioned Applesauce

Applesauce goes well with pork dishes, but try it on the side of turkey or hamburgers. Warm it up and put it on top of vanilla ice cream or just enjoy applesauce all by itself.

(Makes enough for the whole family)

You'll need:
2 pounds cooking apples
1/3 cup water
1/3 cup sugar
cinnamon

1. **STOP** Ask a grown-up to help you peel, core, and slice the apples.

2. Put the apples and water in a heavy pot. **STOP** Tell your grown-up helper to put it on the stovetop over low heat. Let the apples **simmer**, covered, until they are tender.

3. Remove the pot from the heat. Mash apples with a **potato masher**. (Applesauce should be slightly chunky.)

4. Add the sugar and taste the applesauce. If you think it needs it, you can add more sugar.

5. Add cinnamon to taste.

6. Stir well and serve warm.

Pass-Around Potato Salad

Potato salad is a fun alternative to mashed potatoes, french fries, or stuffing.

(Serves 5)

You'll need:

5 red potatoes
1 Tablespoon vinegar
1 Tablespoon olive oil
1/2 cup diced green pepper
1/4 cup diced red onion
1/2 cup mayonnaise
1 teaspoon Dijon-style mustard
1/2 Tablespoon fresh basil, minced
    (or 1/2 teaspoon dried)
1/2 Tablespoon fresh tarragon, minced
    (or 1/2 teaspoon dried)
salt and pepper

1. **STOP** Ask a grown-up to boil the potatoes until you can easily stick them with a fork.

2. Drain the potatoes. Put them in a bowl. Sprinkle with the vinegar and oil. Let them cool.

3. Cut the potatoes into thick slices.

4. Add the peppers and onion.

5. In a small bowl, combine the mayonnaise, mustard, and herbs. Blend together well.

6. Pour the dressing over the potato mixture and toss well.

7. Chill the salad.

Fun Food Fact: Potato chips were invented because of a cranky customer at a restaurant in Saratoga Springs, New York. One night in 1835 at the Moon Lake Lodge, a customer kept sending his french fries back to Chef George Crumb, because they were too thick and soft. Finally, Crumb took a potato, sliced it paper thin, fried it, and personally served the chips to a thrilled customer.

133

Come-and-Get-It Coleslaw

Coleslaw is so *yummy*, you'd never guess it's chock-full of vegetables!

(Serves 8 to 10)

You'll need:
1 head of cabbage
1/2 cup carrot, grated
1/2 cup onion, diced
1 cup mayonnaise
2 Tablespoons vinegar
2 teaspoons sugar
3 Tablespoons plain yogurt

1. With help, shred the cabbage into thin pieces.

2. Combine the cabbage, carrots, and onion. Toss well.

3. In a small bowl, combine the mayonnaise, vinegar, sugar, and yogurt. Mix well.

4. Pour the dressing over the cabbage mixture.

5. Toss well and refrigerate for a few hours.

Fun Food Fact: Did you know wild carrots have flowers? In their second year of growth, they produce clusters of small white flowers that are called "Queen Anne's lace" because people say they look like a lace tablecloth.

Easy Baked French Fries

Baked french fries are much easier to make than the fried kind—
and they're more healthful, too!

(Serves 4)

You'll need:

4 large potatoes
1 Tablespoon white vinegar
4 Tablespoons margarine*
1/4 cup vegetable oil

1. STOP Ask a grown-up to preheat the oven to 400°.

2. STOP You can peel the potatoes, or leave the skins on (but wash them REALLY well if you leave the skins on!).

3. STOP With some help, cut the potatoes into strips, about 1/4" thick.

4. Put the potatoes in a bowl. Add the vinegar and enough water to cover the potatoes so they don't turn brown.

5. Drain the potatoes.

6. Melt the margarine in the microwave. Add the oil and stir.

7. Pour the oil mixture over the potatoes. Toss until the potatoes are coated.

8. Place the potatoes on a cookie sheet.

9. STOP Bake the potatoes at 400° for 35 to 40 minutes until golden. Turn them after about 20 minutes of baking.

*1 stick margarine = 1/2 cup margarine = 8 Tablespoons margarine

Tip: For fries with extra zing, use sweet potatoes in place of regular potatoes!

Fun Food Fact: French fries are NOT from France. "French" means to cut into narrow strips before frying. These frenched potatoes were first made in Belgium in 1876.

Fancy Finales

Everyone knows the best part of dinner is dessert, so don't forget the sweet stuff when you prepare your next meal. Anything can be a dessert: fruit, puddings, cakes, biscuits, and even crackers and cheese. It just depends on what you're in the mood for, and what you have around the house.

If you really get stumped, try one of our dessert recipes. They are all pretty easy to make, and they're all pretty special. Some are traditional after-dinner treats. Others are some interesting ideas that your family will ooh and aah over. And since you are the chef, you don't need to ask permission to lick the bowl!

Tropical Baked Bananas

Mom and Dad will love this simple, healthful snack.

(Serves 1)

You'll need:
1/2 unpeeled banana
sugar
grated coconut
lemon juice
cinnamon

1. **STOP** Ask a grown-up to preheat the oven to 375°.

2. Without removing the peel, cut the banana in half lengthwise.

3. **STOP** Arrange the banana on a cookie sheet and ask your grown-up helper to bake it in its peel for 15 minutes.

4. Peel the skins from the bananas.

5. Sprinkle the banana with your choice of coconut, lemon juice, sugar, and cinnamon.

Careful Cooking: When walking with a knife, always keep the blade pointed down.

Dessert Pizza

Pizza for dessert?! This is the most unique and delicious pizza you'll ever try!

(Serves 6-8)

You'll need:

1 package (18-20 ounces) refrigerated
    cookie dough (chocolate chip or sugar)
one 8-ounce container of
    whipped topping, thawed
2 cups assorted sliced fruit
    (bananas, kiwis, strawberries,
    melon, etc.)

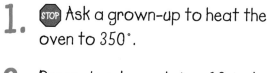
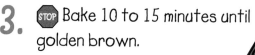

4. When it's cool, place the crust on a serving plate.

5. Spread whipped topping on the cookie crust.

6. Garnish with fruit. Slice and serve.

1. **STOP** Ask a grown-up to heat the oven to 350°.

2. Press dough evenly in a 12-inch pizza pan.

3. **STOP** Bake 10 to 15 minutes until golden brown.

Banana Splitzer

Here's a healthful version of the banana split!

(Serves 2)

You'll need:
1/2 cup plain yogurt
1/2 envelope chocolate pudding mix
1 banana, peeled
1/4 teaspoon lemon juice*
1/4 ounce chopped nuts**
whipped topping
maraschino cherries

1. (STOP) Ask an adult to help you mix the yogurt in a blender for 30 seconds.

2. (STOP) Add the pudding mix and blend for one minute.

3. (STOP) With some help, cut the banana into six slices. Sprinkle with lemon juice.

4. Put 3 slices of banana in each dish. Top each with 1/2 the pudding mixture.

5. Sprinkle both with nuts and top with whipped topping and a cherry.

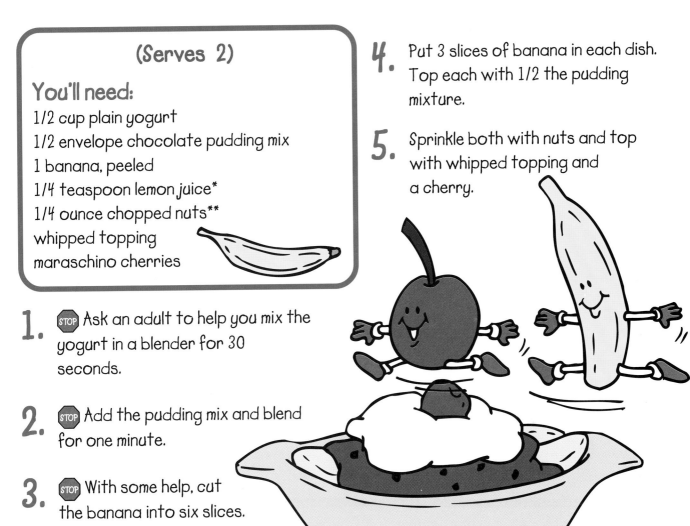

*1 lemon = 3 Tablespoons lemon juice
**4 ounces nuts = 1 cup chopped nuts

Fun Food Fact: The ice cream sundae was invented by a Wisconsin merchant who was running out of ice cream. He did not get a delivery on Sundays, so in 1890, to stretch his ice cream supply, he started serving smaller portions of ice cream on Sunday and topping them with chocolate sauce or fruit syrup. They became so popular, customers started asking for them during the week. The merchant had to change the spelling of the dish though, because townspeople thought a "Sunday Ice Cream" was disrespectful to a holy day.

Lemon Ice Cream

Serve this ice cream with a few vanilla wafers for an elegant ending to any meal.

(Serves 6)

You'll need:
1-1/2 cups sugar
3 cups whipping cream
1/3 cup lemon juice*
1/4 teaspoon salt

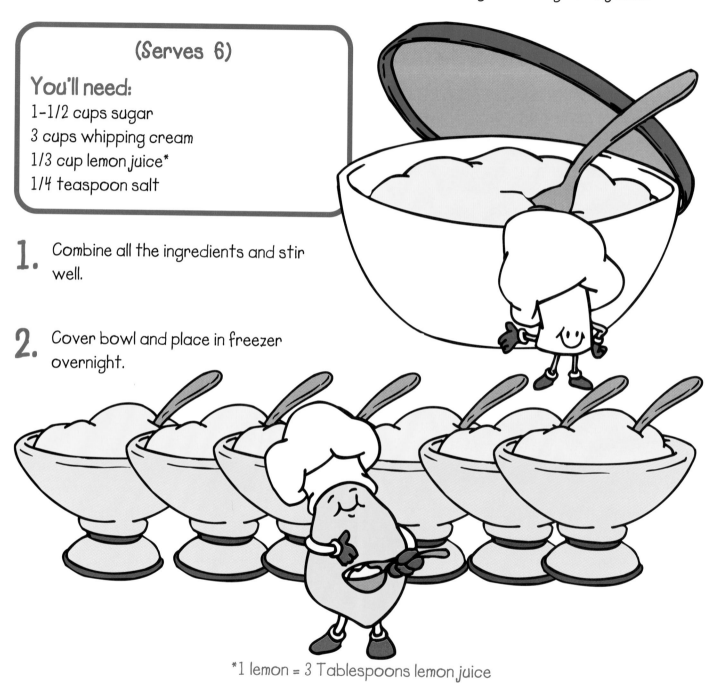

1. Combine all the ingredients and stir well.

2. Cover bowl and place in freezer overnight.

*1 lemon = 3 Tablespoons lemon juice

Fun Food Fact: Ice cream has been around awhile. In the first century A.D. the Roman emperor Nero cooled fruit juices with ice and snow. In the late 1200s, Marco Polo tasted flavored ice in the Far East and told his friends about it. The early English colonists brought ice cream to America in the 1700s, but the first ice cream factory didn't appear until 1851.

Banana Pudding

Try your hand at this version of a popular Southern dessert.

(Serves 4)

You'll need:

12 graham cracker squares
1 Tablespoon plus 1 teaspoon margarine, melted*
1 envelope vanilla pudding mix
2 cups milk
1/2 teaspoon vanilla extract
1 banana, sliced
2 large egg whites
2 Tablespoons sugar

1. **STOP** Ask an adult to preheat the oven to 350°.

2. Spray a 1-1/2 quart casserole dish with nonstick cooking spray.

3. Put graham crackers in a plastic bag and crush them to make crumbs.

4. Combine crumbs and margarine.

5. Press half the crumb mixture into the bottom of the casserole dish.

6. **STOP** Ask your adult helper to bake the crust until firm, three to five minutes. Set aside.

7. **STOP** Increase oven temperature to 425°.

8. Prepare vanilla pudding according to package directions.

9. Stir the vanilla extract into the pudding.

10. Layer half the banana slices over the crust. Top with half the pudding.

11. Repeat layers with the rest of the crumbs, banana, and pudding.

To make meringue:

1. **STOP** In medium bowl, with mixer on high, beat egg whites one minute, until foamy.

2. Gradually add sugar; continue beating on high speed until egg whites are stiff but not dry.

3. Spoon meringue mixture on top of pudding. Smooth meringue with a rubber spatula. **STOP** Ask an adult to bake the pudding until the meringue is golden brown, about five minutes.

*1 stick margarine = 1/2 cup margarine = 8 Tablespoons margarine

Strawberry Shortcake

This is one of the most popular cakes ever.

(Makes 8)

You'll need:

1-3/4 cups all-purpose flour
2 Tablespoons granulated sugar
1 Tablespoon baking powder
3 Tablespoons unsalted butter
    or margarine, cut into pieces*
3/4 cup skim milk
2 pints fresh strawberries, sliced
1 Tablespoon orange juice
1 Tablespoon granulated sugar
whipped topping or fresh whipped cream

1. **STOP** Ask a grown-up to preheat the oven to 450°. Spray a baking sheet with vegetable cooking spray. Set aside.

2. In a bowl, sift together the flour, sugar, and baking powder.

3. Use a whisk or pastry blender to mix the pieces of butter into the flour mixture. Mix it until it begins to look crumbly.

4. Quickly stir in the milk until a soft dough forms.

5. **STOP** With help, roll out the dough until it's about 1/2-inch thick. Using a 2-1/2 inch biscuit cutter (or a drinking glass), cut out biscuits.

6. **STOP** Put the biscuits on the baking sheet. Bake them until they are golden (about 12 to 15 minutes).

7. Place the biscuits on a wire rack to cool.

8. For the filling, combine strawberries, orange juice, and sugar. Mix well.

9. **STOP** With some help, cut the biscuits in half. Place the bottom halves on serving plates. Top each with some filling. Cover with the biscuit tops. Serve with whipped topping.

*1 stick butter = 1/2 cup butter = 8 Tablespoons butter

Fun Food Fact: In Seattle, Washington, in 1994, Biringer Farm Products company made a strawberry shortcake that was 50 feet 3 inches by 8 feet!

Strawberry Whip

This quick and delicious, cool and creamy treat is perfect for a hot summer night.

(Makes 6)

You'll need:

1 pint strawberries
2 Tablespoons honey
1 teaspoon vanilla extract
1 teaspoon grated lemon zest
8 ounces of whipped topping

1. **STOP** Ask a grown-up to help you clean and remove the tops of the strawberries; then chop up half of the strawberries.

2. **STOP** Now ask your helper to put the honey, the vanilla, the zest, and the rest of the strawberries in the blender. Blend until the mixture is smooth.

3. Fold the chopped strawberries and the blended mixture into the whipped topping. Stir to combine. (Do not stir too much; the whipped topping will get too soft.)

4. Spoon into six glasses or serving dishes.

5. Chill until ready to serve.

Mom's Rice Pudding

Rice pudding takes awhile to make, but it's definitely worth the effort!

(Makes 1 large pan)

You'll need:

1 cup long grain white rice
1-1/2 quarts milk
2 eggs
1 cup sugar
1/2 teaspoon vanilla
1 Tablespoon heavy cream
1 Tablespoon melted butter
cinnamon

1. Put the rice in a saucepan and put in enough water to just cover the rice.

2. (STOP) Ask a grown-up to bring the rice to a boil on the stovetop. Boil for two minutes.

3. Add the milk.

4. (STOP) Have your grown-up helper bring the rice mixture to a slow boil, and let it roll for 45 minutes, stirring occasionally.

5. While you are waiting, mix the eggs, sugar, vanilla, cream, and butter in a bowl.

6. Fold the egg mixture into the rice after the rice has "rolled" for 45 minutes.

7. Pour the rice pudding mix into a serving dish or pan. Sprinkle it with cinnamon.

8. Let the pudding cool and then chill it in the refrigerator.

Fun Food Fact: In Manorhaven Park, New York, in 1993, the New York Guild of Chefs made a pot of rice pudding weighing 2,146.6 pounds. The dessert was polished off by over 2,000 people.

Glossary

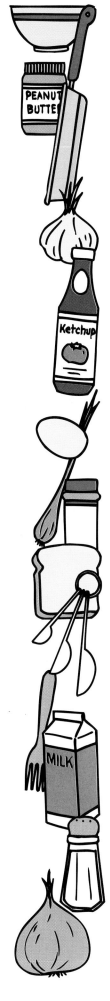

Bake: To cook food inside an oven.

Baking Sheet: A flat pan usually used for baking cookies. Also called a cookie sheet.

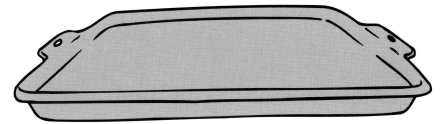

Baste: To keep food from drying out while it cooks by pouring a liquid (like melted butter, water, sauce, or juice) over the top of it.

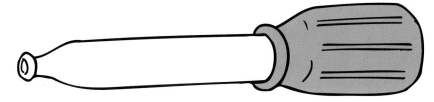

Beat: To mix ingredients quickly with an electric mixer, whisk, or spoon until the mixture is well blended.

Boil: When bubbles are coming to the top of the liquid over and over again, very quickly.

Brown: To cook something, usually with butter or cooking spray, in a pan on the stovetop until the food begins to turn brown or golden.

Glossary

Bundt Pan: A pan with a hole in the middle used for baking a cake.

Casserole Dish: A dish with a lid used for baking things in the oven.

Colander: A container with holes used to drain liquid out of pasta, vegetables, and other items.

Combine: To use a spoon to mix and toss ingredients together.

Cookie Sheet: See Baking Sheet.

146

Glossary

To Cream: Using a spoon or electric mixer to press together and blend ingredients until they are creamy (you usually cream butter and sugar together).

Dash: About 1/16 of a teaspoon (fill a 1/8 teaspoon measure only halfway).

Dice: To cut something into little square pieces.

Double Boiler: A cooking pot in which a smaller pot sits on top of a larger pot. You boil water in the bottom pot, which cooks the mixture on top. It's used to melt chocolate chips, marshmallows, and things like that.

Dredge: To roll a food in a "crumby" mixture like flour or bread crumbs.

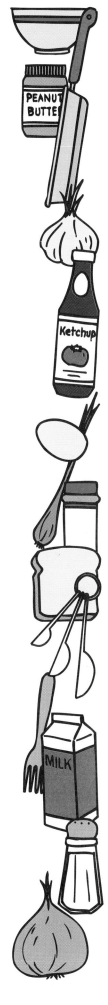

Glossary

Electric Mixer: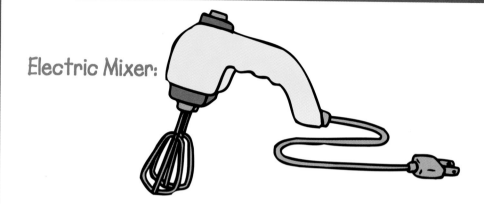

Fold In: To mix ingredients lightly, with a wooden spoon or a rubber spatula. You want the mixture to be fluffy (you will do this a lot with whipped cream) so you just "turn" the ingredient, from the bottom to the top a few times.

Fry: To cook something in an uncovered pot, usually in butter or cooking spray.

Garnish: To decorate food. You can use vegetables, fruit, leaves, or herbs.

To Grease: To rub a coat of shortening, butter, or margarine over a pan so what you are cooking will not stick to it.

Loaf Pan: A rectangle-shaped pan for baking.

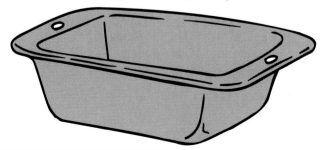

Glossary

Mince: To cut into very tiny pieces.

To Mix: Using a spoon or electric mixer, blend all the ingredients together until the mixture is smooth and even.

Pastry Blender: This tool is used to cut butter up into a flour mixture.

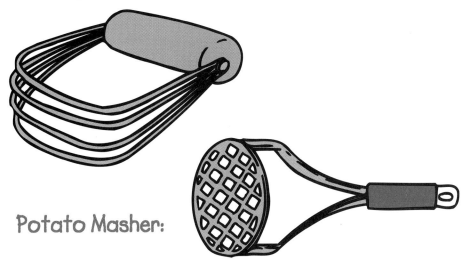

Potato Masher:

To Purée: To put food in a blender or food processor and blend until it is very creamy and smooth.

Rolling Boil: When water is boiling on a stove and the bubbles are coming to the top very fast.

Sauté: To cook something on a stovetop, usually in butter or cooking spray, until it is cooked the way you want it or it starts to turn color.

Glossary

Shred: To cut or pull something apart in thin, uneven strips.

Simmer: To cook a food in some kind of liquid, like water or broth, just below the boiling point. Bubbles come slowly to the top.

Skillet:

Spatula: A tool used for scraping, spreading, and mixing. Also used for flipping things like pancakes and hamburgers.

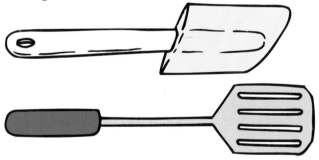

To Strain: When you separate food from the liquid it was cooking in (for example, drain the water out of spaghetti after it is boiled).

Glossary

Thawed: When something that was frozen defrosts.

Whisk: A wire kitchen tool used to beat ingredients until they are well blended and fluffy.

Wire Rack: Used to cool cookies and other foods.

By the Spoonful

Teaspoons	Tablespoons	Cups	Fluid Ounces (to measure liquids)
3 teaspoons	1 Tablespoon		1/2 fluid ounce
6 teaspoons	2 Tablespoons	1/8 cup	1 fluid ounce
12 teaspoons	4 Tablespoons	1/4 cup	2 fluid ounces
16 teaspoons	5 Tablespoons plus 1 teaspoon	1/3 cup	
18 teaspoons	6 Tablespoons	1/3 cup plus 2 teaspoons	3 fluid ounces
24 teaspoons	8 Tablespoons	1/2 cup	4 fluid ounces
32 teaspoons	10 Tablespoons plus 2 teaspoons	2/3 cup	
36 teaspoons	12 Tablespoons	3/4 cup	6 fluid ounces
48 teaspoons	16 Tablespoons	1 cup	8 fluid ounces

By the Cupful

2 cups = 16 fluid ounces = 1 pint

4 cups = 2 pints = 1 quart

4 quarts = 1 gallon

A dash = about 1/16 of a teaspoon
(fill up a 1/8 teaspoon measure halfway)

A pinch = the amount you can grab between your finger and thumb

Ready, SET, Go!

When *your* meal is cooked and *you* are ready to serve, it's time to add the finishing touch. It's time to set the table! Follow the diagram below to be sure everything goes in the right place.

One day, you may feel ready to invite friends over for a fancy dinner. When *you do*, you can set the table for a formal dinner. It will look like this:

Folding Napkins

Do you want to give your table a little bit of pizzazz? Fold your napkins in a special way, and you'll get everyone's attention!

The Bowtie

1. Fold the napkin in half. Fold it in half again, to make a square.
2. Fold two opposite corners so they touch at the center.
3. Fold the napkin to make four equal pleated sections.
4. Tie a ribbon in a bow around the center.

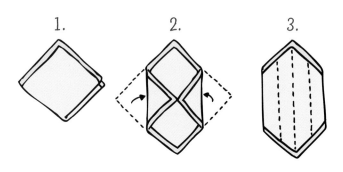

The Fan

1. Fold the napkin in half.
2. Make a fold one inch from the edge. Make a second fold in the opposite direction, one inch from the first fold. Keep doing this until the napkin is completely folded.
3. Place the folded napkin in a glass. Spread out the folds to make a fan.

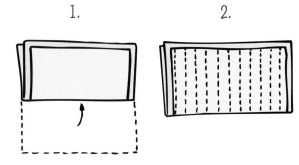

The Sailboat

1. Fold the napkin in half so two opposite corners touch. It will look like a triangle.
2. Fold it in half again.
3. Hold the napkin so the point is at the top.
4. Make a fold one inch from the bottom. Now fold the bottom edge up again.
5. Take the two ends that are sticking out and fold them toward each other. Tuck one end into the other.

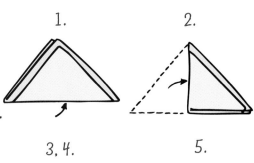

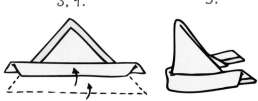

How to Cook Rice

You can always use instant rice to save time when you are cooking, but if you don't have any in your kitchen, don't be nervous about using regular rice. It's as simple as these short steps below:

To cook white rice: Use two times the amount of water as there is white rice. For example, if you are cooking one cup of white rice, combine it with two cups of water. Ask an adult to bring the rice and water to a boil in a saucepan. Reduce the burner to low, cover the pot, and simmer the rice until all the water is gone. This should take about 20 minutes. Take the rice off the stove when it is done, and let the pot stand, with the cover on, for ten minutes. Use a fork to "fluff it up." One cup of uncooked white rice will be three cups once it is cooked.

To cook brown rice: Cook brown rice the same as white rice, but use 2-1/2 times the amount of water as there is rice. For example, if you use one cup of brown rice, you will use 2-1/2 cups of water. Brown rice will take about 30 minutes instead of 20 for the water to be absorbed. One cup of uncooked brown rice will give you about 2-1/2 cups once it is cooked.

How to Cook Spaghetti and Other Pastas:

1. How much pasta? Two ounces of dry pasta or three ounces fresh pasta is needed for each serving. Each of those will make one cup of cooked pasta. A bunch of spaghetti that is 1-1/2 inches around will serve four people.

1¹/₂"

2. What kind of a pot? The cooking pot does not have to be wide around, but it should be deep.

3. How much water? Use about two quarts of water for every eight ounces of pasta.

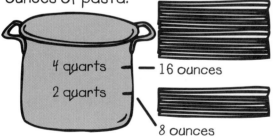

4 quarts — 16 ounces
2 quarts
8 ounces

4. When do I put the pasta in? Put the pasta in the water once it begins to boil.

5. Do I need to add anything to the water? You don't need to add anything. A spoonful of olive oil may be added to keep the pasta from sticking together.

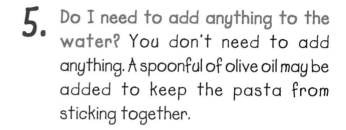

6. Do I have to stir the pasta? Stir the pasta once, when you first put it in, but then just let it cook.

7. How do I know when it is done? If you break a piece in half and it is still white in the middle, it's not done. Most store-bought dried pastas will take 8 to 12 minutes.

8. What do I do when it's done? Drain the pasta in a colander, into the sink.

INDEX OF RECIPES

The stars following each recipe name is the recipe's chef's hat rating.

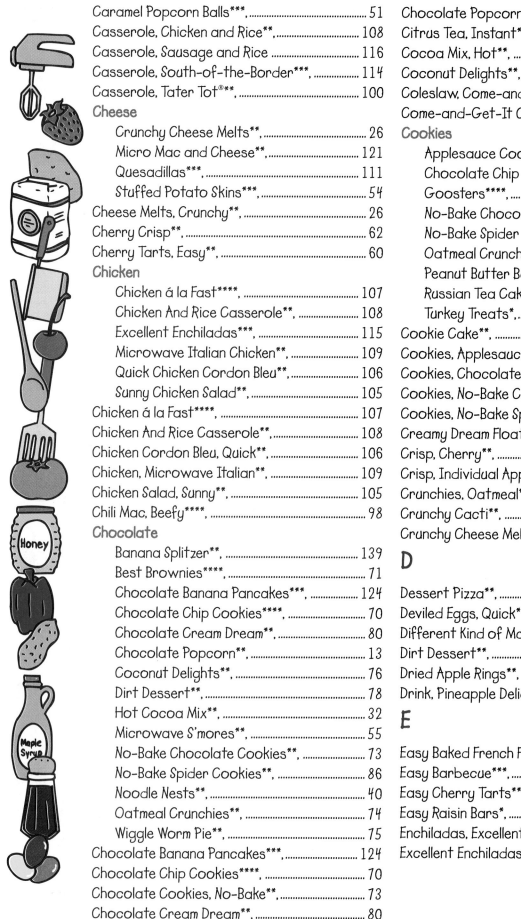

D

E